D1580553

PSYCHE SPEAKS

A Jungian Approach to Self and World

♦

Russell Arthur Lockhart

CHIRON PUBLICATIONS

Wilmette, Illinois

Psyche Speaks

THE C. G. JUNG LECTURES

Inaugural Series

1982

Sponsored by

THE C. G. JUNG FOUNDATION FOR ANALYTICAL PSYCHOLOGY, Inc.

New York, NY

The Chiron Monograph Series, Volume I

General Editors: Nathan Schwartz-Salant, Murray Stein
Managing Editor: Harriet Hudnut Halliday

International Standard Book Number: 0-933029-28-4;
0-933029-22-5 (pbk.)

Library of Congress Catalog Card Number: 87-18260

Printed in the United States of America

Typeset by The Lockhart Press

Book design by Kirk G. Panikis

Grateful acknowledgement is made for the following permissions:
C. G. Jung, *Word and Image,* ed. Aniela Jaffé, Bollingen Series XCVII: Vol. 2. Copyright © 1979 by Princeton University Press. Fig. 181 reprinted with permission of Princeton University Press.
"The Restored" by Theodore Roethke copyright © 1960 by Beatrice Roethke as Administratrix of the Estate of Theodore Roethke from THE COLLECTED POEMS OF THEODORE ROETHKE. Reprinted by permission of Doubleday & Company, Inc.
The complete poem, "Casida of the Rose," trans. Robert Bly, *News of the Universe* (San Francisco: Sierra Club Books, 1980), p. 109. Reprinted with permission.
Material from *Candle of Vision* reprinted by arrangement with University Books Inc., Secaucus, New Jersey.
"Created and Abandoned," by Muriel Spark, reprinted by permission of Harold Ober Associates Incorporated. Copyright © 1979 by Copyright Administration Limited. First published in *The New Yorker.*
Sonnett II (p. 197) from SELECTED POEMS OF RAINER MARIA RILKE translated by Robert Bly. Copyright © 1981 by Robert Bly. Reprinted by permission of Harper & Row, Publishers, Inc.
The complete poem V from "Proverbs and Songs," from THE DREAM BELOW THE SUN, Selected Poems of Antonio Machado copyright © 1981 by Willis Barnstone, The Crossing Press, Freedom, Cal. Reprinted with permission.
Jose Clemento Orozco (1883–1949), Mexican; The Epic of American Civilization, 1932–4, Panel #12, Gods of the Modern World, Fresco, P.934.13, Courtesy of the Trustees of Dartmouth College, Hanover, N.H.

Library of Congress Cataloging-in-Publication Data

Lockhart, Russell A., 1938–
    Psyche speaks.

    Bibliography: p.
    Includes index.
    1. Imagery (Psychology)   2. Psychoanalysis.
3. Jung, C.G. (Carl Gustav), 1875–1961.   I. Title.
[DNLM: 1. Dreams—essays.   2. Psychoanalysis—essays.
WM 460.5.D8 L816p]
BF367.L63   1987   154   87-18260
ISBN 0-933029-28-4
ISBN 0-933029-22-5 (pbk.)

To

Allen Spiegel,

shot and killed,
at seventeen,
outside the House of Donuts,
Forty-Second & Madison Avenue,
New York City,
October 24, 1981,

... right before my eyes.

Contents

Acknowledgments

I SEND THIS BOOK into the world with deep appreciation for the kindness of the Lecture Committee of the C. G. Jung Foundation for Analytical Psychology, the Barker Foundation, and particularly Philip and Beverly Zabriskie, for extending to me the invitation to inaugurate the C. G. Jung Lectures. I trust this offering begins to repay their confidence in me to meet the challenge such an obligation engendered. I want to thank many individuals—here unnamed—who have read these pages in earlier forms and through correspondence and discussion have provided me with inspiration not only to see this work into print but to improve it substantially. Still, my obstinance has precluded many valuable suggestions from finding their way into these pages. To my wife and children I offer my apologies for too much absence while these lectures and this book stole my time and energy. Their love, encouragement, and humor have made this work possible. I'm very grateful to Hope Fletcher for her work on the manuscript and on the index, and especially to Holly Halliday, who with her editor's eye and pencil has purged this work of all the errors I could no longer see. What errors remain in content or form are mine alone. And, finally, I wish to thank the following, for their generous permission to use copyrighted material: Robert Bly, The Crossing Press, Doubleday and Co., Harper and Row, Harold Ober and Associates, Penguin Books, Princeton University Press, Theosophical Publishing House, and the Trustees of Dartmouth College.

Preface

I T IS FIVE YEARS NOW since I delivered the lectures here set down in print for the first time. In contrast to other things I have written, where revision and rewriting preparatory to publication have always been quite easy for me to accomplish, these lectures have curiously resisted all my attempts to "make a book" of them. For reasons I do not know, but cannot deny, the lectures seemed to want publication as I gave them on those three spring evenings in 1982, in the lecture hall at the New York Blood Center. The C. G. Jung Foundation had made special arrangements with a taping firm to record the lectures, but the firm discovered to its chagrin that the master tape was filled with static over my voice and the tapes proved useless. I have been content to let the matter rest and allow the lectures their "silence." Still, I have been encouraged often during these past few years to make them more available than the few now-worn typescript copies that have circulated privately. It is this steady prompting that I find myself responding to now, for in many respects I feel embarrassed about this "failure" to make a book of the material only hinted at in these lectures. Perhaps that will come later. In the meantime, I must express a deep and profound appreciation to my friends and colleagues Murray Stein and Nathan Schwartz-Salant for gently goading me to let these lectures see the printed page and for their granting me the opportunity to publish them in basically their original form. Even so, I must ask the reader's indulgence. Read what follows as if I were talking to you, sitting perhaps in some wooded place, with animals watching, their ears pricked up as if they were hearing something, something hiding in the words.

PART ONE:

Where Madness is Psyche's Only Nurse

What the dream, which is not manufactured by us, says is *just so*.

— C. G. Jung

Introduction

I FLEW ACROSS THE COUNTRY sitting next to an elderly rabbi who had been lecturing in San Francisco. When he discovered I was to lecture in New York, he told me, in the most fatherly way, I must have at least one joke and one story. That way, no matter what happened, people wouldn't be cheated for, as he said, the essential things in life are humor and story telling. I told him I was terrible at remembering jokes but asked if he had one I might use. Oh, yes! And he gave me a joke. I had heard the joke a short time before and this odd synchrony was sufficient to convince me that this was the joke I would tell. The more I reflected on the joke the more I sensed why it belonged to the theme of my lectures. That I will not tell—you must guess it. But I will tell the joke.

> An airplane comes in for a landing, everyone tightly buckled in their seats. Just as the wheels touch the ground the plane began screeching. It came to a sudden stop wrenching everyone so violently they were nearly cut in half so quick was the stop. The pilot exclaimed: "That's the shortest damn runway I've ever seen." And the copilot, looking out the window, answered: "Yep, but it sure is wide."

The rabbi, being somewhat familiar with Jungian psychology, asked me what was new in Jungian circles. After determining that he wanted my actual opinion and not just the latest gossip, I told

3

him there were three areas that were very active. One area concerned relating Jungian psychology to other depth psychologies. This was particularly pronounced in the area of borderline and narcissistic personality disorders. I mentioned Nathan Schwartz-Salant's book, *Narcissism and Character Transformation*,[1] as an exquisite example. This book exemplifies what is possible when the many fine and subtle threads of a mythic pattern are attended to, in contrast to the more usual approach of basing an entire psychological system on a single abstracted element of a myth. As an expert on the Torah, the rabbi greatly appreciated this idea.

Then I mentioned the burgeoning field I called "a modern celebration of the goddess," consisting of many attempts to renew and revitalize the feminine spirit, and in particular to rescue the feminine from its imprisonment in the stolid anima psychology of the patriarchy. I told the rabbi of the marvelous flowering of books and papers by woman writers and confided to him that I was jealous of these women with their books all finished, jealous because I found myself unexpectedly mired in and entangled in concern for the relevance of books in our time—and me the owner of 10,000 books and trying to write one!

Then I told the rabbi there was a great deal of energetic work in an area James Hillman had christened *archetypal* psychology,[2] an approach that works principally through methods of imaginal revisioning, an approach finding sympathetic resonance in widespread revisioning efforts in theology, literature, and the arts.

These were not the only edges of current development in what is broadly conceived as Jungian psychology but they seemed to me the most active edges and certainly the most visible. And where was I in all of this? the rabbi wanted to know. I told him I didn't find integrating Jungian and other depth psychologies of any particular interest to me. It was my perception that too much of what I valued in Jung's psychology got *lost* in this pursual of rapprochement with our psychoanalytic brothers and sisters. I told the rabbi I had more interest in and feeling for the efforts at resurrecting and revitalizing images of the feminine. All the emphasis on what has been abandoned, neglected, and devalued seemed focused too narrowly on the feminine and too rooted in images from the past. I told him I felt there was need of a similar redemption of the masculine spirit and that without this the feminine would wander alone, and this will not suffice. I told him what needs most attention is the psyche itself, not in terms of how it can be *interpreted* in images from the past (whether a person's past or a culture's past), but how one can relate to and participate in the manifestations of what the psyche is pointing to in the future. And what does the future hold? the rabbi asked. I told him I felt our time was pregnant with the possibilities of *eros* and that our future concerns will be centered on the eros problem not only in Jungian psychology but throughout our culture.

And while I find great resonance and comradery in the work of James Hillman and the many others working within an archetypal and revisioning frame, my feeling once again pushes not so much for revisioning what has been, but for a *return of vision* to the *heart* of everything we are and everything we do. I share the romantic's dream that it is the imagination *embodied* in this world that is worth what Jung meant when he said that "all steps forward in the improvement of the human psyche have been paid for by blood."[3] Yet, I found myself telling the rabbi that even payment in blood no longer distinguishes advancing or regressing in our time. Blood alone will not suffice. We need *something else.*

Psyche Speaks, as a book, I told the rabbi, had taken a rather odd turn. It had become a repository, a collection, an odd assortment of psychic images in the form of dreams, visions, fantasies, and synchronicities about the world, about relationship, about our psychology. What distinguished this strange collection was that no attempt was made to interpret the material in terms of psychology. Rather, the intention was reversed. The psychic material was used to interpret the world, relationship, psychology. But not so much interpretation as a kind of *weaving* with the images, an attempt to focus on what psyche says directly. For as Jung made clear, a dream and what it says are *just so.*[4] We so quickly go into an interpretative style that we often forget that the unconscious can say exactly what it desires to say, that psyche's speech can be quite autonomous, that often, like a good story, a compelling poem, a joke even, the dream desires simply to be told and heard. But what does this accomplish? asked the rabbi. I was getting a bit passionate about what I was saying and his question brought me to tell the rabbi a little story as a trade for his joke.

> It seems a would-be composer came to Mozart seeking his advice. "How do I write symphonies?" Mozart replied: "Well, you are young yet; I think you should begin by composing minuets." The young man was greatly annoyed and exclaimed: "But you were writing symphonies when you were nine years old!" "Yes," Mozart responded, "but I didn't ask anyone how to do it."

The plight of this young man is familiar to each of us. I can't imagine any of us would bother with psychological lectures or reading psychological essays if we didn't have to ask how to do it. We would be *doing* it! How much truer for the lecturer, the essayist. Even worse: the lecturer is often seized by yet a third character, voicing itself in the manner of an interpreter or critic who cannot bring himself to admit of any desire to write symphonies, certainly hasn't and never will write symphonies, yet somehow possesses an amazing capacity to know what's wrong with symphonies others have written and is absolutely certain what sort of symphonies ought to be written!

The most agonizing thing about this little Mozart story is that Mozart was not speaking from inflation, but from simple and truthful modesty. The reason Mozart didn't have to ask anyone how to write symphonies is that symphonies *presented* themselves to him: invented, enlarged, produced all at once in what he described as "lively dreams,"[5] dreams that were so forceful Mozart had to stop what he was otherwise doing and write out what he heard—almost as if something *beyond* Mozart's consciousness desired these symphonies to be written. We might call this the *presentational* psyche. In spite of our myriad experience in the matter, the reality of autonomous desire on the part of the presentational psyche remains strange, mysterious, and clouded with doubt.

Mozart devoted his willful energies to crafting those lively dreams into the actualities we love to hear. In this he was an artist. In his listening, taking that autonomous world seriously, considering it, caring for it, tending it, submitting himself to it, and most of all committing himself to making it *real* by giving it *body* in this world—in this Mozart was following a *genius*. I mean genius in the old sense: an *inborn tutelary spirit*. Opening one's ears to this source of unique and healing speech from the "unconscious chambers of the soul"[6] requires a kind of genius—or a lot less of what we have come to call civilization. It is a genius we lose contact with easily in the pursuit of our everyday lives, as if we were always and forever *pursuing* our life rather than *living* it.

We know that the psychic source that caught Mozart's ear, the *presentational* unconscious, produces not only symphonies but an endless and natural flowering of images. These images come into our awareness in such a way that impersonal qualities interpenetrate and mix together with personal qualities to produce the highly unique and individual realities that form the texture of dream and vision. Alas, it is difficult to hear this deeper speech of psyche over the loud shoutings of all those amazing claims upon our attention and allegiance which constitute the bulk of our experience.

How I would love to speak as psyche speaks! Then I wouldn't be chained to talking *about* it. But what would that be? Two compelling fantasies have hounded me. The first was literally to let psyche speak: dreams, visions, wild synchronicities, and psychopathologies of everyday life—mine and others all mixed together without commentary, interpretation, analysis, and endless babble about meaning. A genuine theater of the soul! Can you imagine what madness that would be? The second fantasy was to be completely silent. Imagine: complete silence, to listen to what the spontaneous psyche would say when no one was going on and on *about* psyche's speech.

Recall André Gregory's comment that we are becoming so anesthetized that it won't be long before we will pay $10,000 to be castrated just to *feel* something.[7] I can sooner imagine a time when we will pay a lot of money to seek *silence*. And unless one finds a bit of silence, there is little hope of hearing psyche's speech until it too becomes the clamor and clang of nightmare, accident, sickness, or madness. Even in Wordsworth's time, he would complain that psyche was shut out because "the world is too much with us."[8] It is so true today we do not know it.

Yet, until I work up the courage to actually do one or the other of these things, or until you, rising up in rebellion at so many words, demand it, I will resign myself reluctantly to the role of talking *about*, realizing full well that we are far removed from any essential mystery when we do this. Realizing too, however, that in our culture one does not get paid for having or telling dreams— only for explaining, interpreting, and teaching about them. In that and in deeper ways as we shall see, dreams and poems, dreamers and poets, share a similar fate. This may be a blessing in disguise, for perhaps only in dreams and poems can we experience a freedom from the corrosively consumptive claim of money's power—this being the most powerful way in which "the world is too much with us" in our time.

I dare to hope at least the *echoes* of psyche's speech reach you, the reader. I don't mean those disembodied echoes that find their origin in the realm of Narcissus, but in those singing bits and pieces of still living flesh and blood of that other virginal Echo, torn and scattered by Pan's frenzied herdsmen, the Echo who found her home in the ground of mother earth, the Echo who is always singing the speech of gods, of mortals, of organs, of beasts, of stones, of speech itself in her own song, *that* sense of Echo as the deeper voice of all things.[9]

As victims of a strikingly noisy culture, there may even be a yearning to hear *something else*. Still, someone said it was difficult for a painter to speak to an audience because people would listen with their minds and not with their hands. When it comes to psyche's speech, I know we listen so quickly with our minds that we forget to hear. We don't give psyche's speech time *to wander* in the labyrinth of the ear.

The Forgotten Psyche

TO INTRODUCE what I will be wandering through—and I must warn you I will be wandering—it will be helpful first to tell where I've been wandering already. The image of labyrinth feels exact: I grasp the thread running through this work I've done, yet I cannot tell whether the thread leads me toward that *something else* or more deeply into the confines of a dead-end maze.

Fifteen years ago, I began working on a theme triggered by seeing Stanley Kubrick's film of Anthony Burgess's novel, *A Clockwork Orange*. At that time, I was engaged in a close reading of Jung's autobiography, *Memories, Dreams, Reflections*. One paragraph stood out as absolutely crucial and affected me so strongly I wrote it out and pasted it to my dream book so I would see it regularly. Jung wrote:

> I took great care to try to understand every single image, every item of my psychic inventory, and to classify them scientifically—so far as this was possible—and above all, to realize them in actual life. That is what we usually neglect to do. We allow the images to rise up, and maybe wonder about them, but that is all. We do not take the trouble to understand them, let alone draw ethical conclusions from them. This stopping-short conjures up the negative effects of the unconscious.
>
> It is equally a grave mistake to think that it is enough to gain some understanding of the images and that knowledge can here make a halt. Insight into them must be converted into an ethical obligation. Not to do so is to fall prey to the power principle, and

> this produces dangerous effects which are destructive not only to
> others but even to the knower. The images of the unconscious place
> a great responsibility upon a man. Failure to understand them, or a
> shirking of ethical responsibility, deprives him of his wholeness and
> imposes a painful fragmentariness on his life.[10]

Almost everything that is important to me in Jung's psychology is implicit in this paragraph. I saw all those painful difficulties in myself. I experienced in too many ways my own frequent failure to convert images I experienced and struggled to understand into ethical obligations enacted in life. Even so, I was fascinated by Jung's belief that it was the *unconscious* that placed such a great responsibility upon a person. Psychology, even the *Jungian* psychology I knew personally and professionally, seemed to picture the principle burdens elsewhere and, to the extent that the images of the unconscious were listened to and understood, they seemed to be used more for purposes of alleviating burdens, solving problems, and generally oriented toward helping the ego to develop, to reconstruct, to become conscious, to withdraw projections, to integrate the shadow. And, of course, there can be no undervaluing or escaping the utter necessity of this work. Everything I will say here presupposes this process of *completing* the ego. The union of the ego with its other side, the shadow, is inescapable psychological work. Even so, for me the deepest question became: what does a relatively integrated and conscious ego *do*?

I sensed in Jung's statement that even the completed ego would remain in painful fragmentariness and be subject to power problems if the *intentions* of the deeper and autonomous unconscious—what I imagined he meant by the "great responsibility"—were forgotten and not realized in life. This pointed to Jung's fundamental interest in the task of *incarnating* the Self, that is, bringing the Self into flesh-and-blood reality, in this world, in this time. This incarnation relativizes the ego, casting it out of center place. In my view, this incarnation necessarily involves the ego in three essential tasks. *First*: perceiving the Self as distinct from ego's unconsciousness. *Second*: exercising conscious choice in discriminating the paradoxical nature of the Self as distinct from ego's tendencies toward possession, passivity, and identification.

Third: realizing the Self in lived life as distinct from exclusive realization of the secular demands of the ego.

For Jung, the directing center of lived life, then, is not the ego but elsewhere. The location of this elsewhere and the genesis of its contents are indeterminate. What Jung called the *symbolic life* is life directed by the symbol. In this sense, the symbol is not an intellectual or conceptual understanding, but an engine pushing for realization and manifestation in this life, in this world. Exactly what is being pushed for is indeterminate because the symbol carries the unknown future. It is this incarnation of symbolic realities, which cannot be known by the ego fully in advance, which have their origin "elsewhere," that places such an enormous responsibility upon the ego as both an instrument and cross of this incarnation. It is just this factor that causes us such unease when we talk about Jung's psychology—or at least his sense of psyche—as being fundamentally *religious*. Put another way, Jung's work points toward the ego's conscious participation in the birth of a modern myth, a myth incarnating a mystery we do not know.

Our psychological work on ego development, reconstruction, and integration of the shadow may be amenable to a scientific description, teachable technique, methods that can be mastered— may even allow a kind of rapprochement among the different depth-psychoanalytic perspectives. But the issue of the ego consciously committing itself to the symbolic life is *not* a scientific question. It is a question of initiation and ritual. It is a *way of life* having more in common with religious and artistic traditions than with science. Confusing these two aspects of Jung's psychology is responsible for many of our muddles.

Well, of course, this is easier to talk about than to do. But more than that: *it is easy to forget.* And it was because I had such a terrible time remembering this fundamental fact at the heart of what to me is meant by *Jungian,* that I committed myself not only in my personal life but in my professional life as well to what I called *the forgotten psyche.* It seemed to me that one was easily seduced into believing and then acting upon the idea that individuation means *wholeness of the ego* and then forgetting that this work of healing and completing the ego—although absolutely crucial and necessary—is for a deeper and larger purpose: the realization of those images of the unconscious that Jung described as the "great experiment of the psyche."[11]

The most blatant example of forgetting psyche is to be found in psychotherapy's purely behavioral approaches, where psyche's *voice in symptoms* is not heard. In my first essay, called "The Forgotten Psyche of Behavioral Therapy,"[12] I described the dreams of a woman who had undergone behavioral treatment and had been relieved of her disturbing symptoms. From the dreams I sensed that through the cure, psyche's voice had become muted, and I expressed the opinion that to deprive an individual of symptoms may reflect an unarguable humanistic impulse to relieve suffering, but it may cost the individual a rare and unique opportunity to learn the deeper meaning of life.

Then I noticed a general failure to listen to the *voices of madness*. In an essay titled, "Mary's Dog is an Ear Mother"[13] I illustrated the idea that in the realms of psychosis we are not hearing some foreign language from a far-off alien land, but as Jung put it, "we are looking at the very foundations of our own being, the matrix of those vital problems on which we are all engaged."[14] In the hospital were I was working, and in nearly all psychiatric and psychological approaches to madness, and even more so in the world generally, everyone seemed to be doing their utmost not to listen to what is said there in those voices of psychosis. I felt that my patient's statement, "Mary's dog is an ear mother," was not to be discounted as meaningless madness. Rather, it was what I would now call a kind of poetry. If one lets such speech into one's ears, this speech begins to stir that deeper matrix Jung mentioned, and one will begin to hear psyche speak back in the mother-ground of the ear. We are afraid to hear not only the mad speech of others, but our own mad speech as well. In our sophistication we deaden our ears, losing capacity to listen innocently. *Innocent* ears means, quite literally, ears *not dead*. We need innocent ears, ears alive.

The poet's madness and the madness of the psychotic have often been linked and we have something to learn not only from this linking, but also that in our modern culture the poet's voice is nearly forgotten and unheard as well. To my ears, my patient's psyche was speaking of an emerging possibility in relating to the psyche: that the animal side of Mary (the body of the feminine), if not denied, would become the mother-ground for innocent ears—a new way to hear psyche's speech.

So, I turned my attention to the *voices of the body* in their most ineluctable physical form: disease and illness. In an essay called "Cancer in Myth and Dream,"[15] I worked on the necessity of hearing what psyche says even in that most difficult of physical illnesses we call cancer. Not listening to the psyche can be seen as an important factor in the emergence of cancer as well as most disease and sickness. And, while no degree of listening can ever completely overrule the autonomous workings of the body, it is clear that listening to psyche can play a helpful part in treatment as well.

Then it seemed to me that one of the places we hear psyche least is in the many *voices of relationship*. It is here that the wounded and wounding ego speaks loudest of all. In my own experience of relationship difficulties, and in dealing with the myriad phenomena of relationship in others, I found that the most crucial problems of relationship stemmed most often from *not telling*. In working out the implications of this in an essay called "Eros in Language, Myth and Dream,"[16] I came to the conclusion that *eros means telling,* and that an eros relationship means that one is able to tell the other person the *reality* of one's experience over its full range and to tell it in a *personal* way. We often hesitate to tell for fear that we will hurt the other person, or that the other person cannot take it, or will take it wrongly, or will run away. That is when we *wrongfully* wound another person. That is cruelty. *The most cruel thing we do is withhold our reality from one another.*

Then a dream forced upon me the realization that we do not hear psyche's speech at all in our words, that our words are deeply encrusted with ego's frenzied and faddish babble. This dream became a task, and I have made considerable effort to show, as that dream said, that *words are eggs,* and in an essay by that title I urged an eros relationship to words by following the connections that come imaginally when we break the shell of words by attending to the etymological roots of words, whereby the hidden psyche in words can be awakened and freed.[17]

Next came a patient's dream, a voice that announced: "Psyche is hidden by the skin of everyday life." Working on that dream became the essay, "Psyche in Hiding,"[18] an initial attempt to plumb the depths of that expression. Taking off from the prosaic definition of skin as "a tissue forming an external covering," I found myself exploring the secret of Lewis Carroll's *Through the Looking Glass*.[19] I believe this book is the best example of an eros relation to the psyche in the English literature. By exploring the etymological roots and branchings of images hidden in the word "tissue," I found that at the base of the fabric of everyday life is an image of begetting, an image of making a child. That is, of course, the very fabric of everyday life. Imagining on this further, one comes to something else. It is that everyday life itself can beget the child, the new thing, the wonder. By pursuing the underground of the word "tissue" it was possible to recover several pieces of the psyche's forgotten speech: skin as fine cloth, as fine gauze, as entryway through the mirror; skin as entrapping web; skin as subtle thread; skin as architect, as art, as craft, as skill; skin as technique, technology, as technical; skin as begetter; skin as child. Clearly, everyday life is a vast resource for psyche's speech if one can find the ears to hear it. Kandinski says it best: "Everything that is dead quivers. Not only the things of poetry, stars, moon, wood, flowers, but even a white trouser button glittering out of a puddle in the street....Everything has a secret soul, which is silent more often than it speaks."[20]

Next I was turned to that most everyday of everyday realities: *money*. In "Coins and Psychological Change,"[21] I tried to demonstrate that money is the most powerful, practical, and experienced form of transformation—money can be turned into most anything, and that most deeply, money is a talisman of the Self. In this work I discovered that the words "Self," "ethics," and "secret" are inescapably intertwined. Following the lead of these words, I argued that the deeper purpose of secrecy is not to cover up what the ego wants to hide, but to bring the ego into connection with the Self, where, in secret, it comes to learn of its ethical obligations. And, I took a step beyond my earlier formulation that *eros means telling*, by seeing that the ego's unconsciousness heals frequently through revelation and telling of secrets, but that the secret connection with the Self is revealed through *enactment* of the ethical obligations learned and remembered in secret consort with the Self. What is done with money, more that what is said about money, reveals the full reality of our ethical relation to Self.

The earlier idea that eros means telling was now broadened to include *eros as enactment.* And, given this, it was evident that it is this ethical relation to the Self that binds us together as a community. It is what we promise ourselves, each other, and to those who seek our help. What we do with the fruits of our soul work— that hard cold cash—has much to tell us about our relation to the Self, our relation to telos, our relation to the "necessities of soul." This money comes to us marked, marked with the soul struggles of the "other." It does not come clean, but bloodied in the enormous battles of another's soul. Money is another kind of blood and when it circulates through our hands it comes perhaps with more than we care to know. What we do every day with money reflects the state of the ego's relation to its ethical obligations to the Self—those "great responsibilities" Jung spoke of.

And then, in a still unfinished essay that begins to explore the *necessity* of enactment in relation to dreams, I express these thoughts:

> The felt meaningfulness and sense of value of associations, amplifications, and interpretations of dream imagery is not to be confused with an understanding of our relationship to the *uniqueness* of the dream. Certainly the dream may be understood as yet another event or instance in some known mythological context, whether that may be the mythology of the dreamer's past or the culture's past, much in the same sense that a theory such as Freud's Oedipal theory, can be seen not as explanation, but as yet another telling of the Oedipal drama complete with its specific rituals for enactment and dramatic performance. Depth psychology is after all a kind of theatre. But closer to the truth is that the dream embodies the psyche's urge toward new tellings, new stories, new myths. Contextual amplifications and association bring to the dream images what *has been.* The dream also tells what is *coming.* Pindar told of this when he wrote: "The soul slumbers while the body is active; but when the body slumbers, she shows forth in many a vision, the approaching issues of woe and weal." The dream then may embody the future

and this germ of what approaches may be missed if we focus too exclusively on the record of the past. The dream calls out not so much for interpretation as for *relationship,* and that will be found not only in its telling but in what one *does* in response to the dream. Meaning would then be experienced not only as something formulated in words, but as something enacted. Meaning would be achieved not through reflection only, but through enactment of the psyche's urge toward manifestation.[22]

This is the labyrinth I've been wandering through, and with this glance over my shoulder accomplished, it is time to take the next step.

Something Else

I WISH I COULD gather together the right words to express to my generous friends of the Jung and Barker Foundations my thanks for their trust in extending to me their invitation to inaugurate the C.G. Jung Lectures. Of course, it is an honor and a privilege to be put into such a position. Or so it seemed to me when I accepted the invitation in a weakened moment of hubristic courage. It would take all of three lectures to tell the story of the burden, the weight, and the degree to which my accepting this responsibility precipitated a process of unexpected crises, changes, and challenges, not only in my analytic work and teaching but in most every dimension of my life.

During this period, I left my position as a university research professor, left a research field of some twenty years duration, left my position as director of training at the Jung Institute in Los Angeles, left my various involvements in the professional psychological community, left Los Angeles itself, my home for forty-three years. An over-full practice became a skeleton. A once demanding speaking and teaching calendar became empty as I began saying no to all requests. I found myself with my family in the woods in Northern California at the edge of a river surrounded by and towered over by pines and redwoods.[23] For a city boy used to the frenzied life in the big city these were changes!

But now I know what the poet John Ashbery means when he says:

> All around us an extraordinary effort is being made.
> Something is in the air. The tops of the trees are trying
> To speak to this. The audience for these events is amazed,
> Can't believe them, yet is walking in its sleep.[24]

I know now in ways I did not before why our word *truth* comes from the same root as the word *tree*. Yet the most startling change of all was a repeating refrain in my dreams: *No Jungian lectures!* It was too late to say no. Not the least of my burdens was ever-deepening doubts that whatever I would say could satisfy the intention of the C.G. Jung Lectures, namely that "...the Lectures shall make an original contribution to the body of knowledge which is grounded in Jungian psychology, which furthers Jung's ideas, and which expands the range of available literature" and which "...enhances the continuing work of analytical psychology."[25] Wouldn't that require a *Jungian* lecture? Whatever conscious intentions I had in attempting such a grand task were constantly undermined and redirected. I am not trying to be fashionably modest, nor am I apologizing for a kind of failure in advance.

On the contrary, it seems to me that in honoring Dr. Jung yet again for his insistence and commitment to the value of the whole human being, that is, to the infusion of *psychic* reality throughout everything that one is and does, that in taking up this work in Jung's honor, it was fitting that the actual life of the worker, that is *my* life, was transformed. For that, thanks cannot suffice. I trust this psychoactive gift with its unforseen consequences will bear more fruit than the beginning offering I bring here in return.

Still, I feel what must have hounded the old alchemists: that the lead they labored over with such care and devotion, such concern and consideration, remained, after all, lead! That changing themselves didn't suffice. What I have labored to bring to fruition in these lectures remains, I fear, all too leaden. Yet, there has been in the working, in the long hours of struggling over the lead, of suffering inarticulation in the face of things deeply felt, *something else*, and it is this something else that I should like to work myself up to in what follows.

The Dream Wants a Dream

M
Y INTEREST in what I want to tell you began a few years ago when I was listening to Robert Bly play his dulcimer and sing out some poems. Actually, it began earlier. Perhaps in that urgent conference with the principal of my junior high school where my parents were told how worried my writing teacher was about me because of the dark and somber poems I was writing about the Korean War, poems more concerned with death and dying and nuclear nightmare than with the patriotic fervor she thought ought to be the proper concern of a twelve-year-old boy. She called me a "brown study." I don't suppose I endeared myself to her when I corrected her: "black study," I said in quiet defiance.

Perhaps it began earlier in that happier time of grade school when my very first poem was selected for publication in a book I vaguely remember as *Childhood Poems and Other Odd Things.* It was a little limerick that went this way:

> I once had a cow named Madie
> It looked like my old wife Sadie
> To give milk it wouldn't
> I found out it couldn't
> For Madie was not a ladie!

I was eight years old and had begun attending to such differences. Well, no need to trace any further. Certainly, something

19

began in earnest that night I heard Bly speak out these lines of Lorca's wonderful poem, *Casida of the Rose*:

> The rose
> was not searching for the sunrise:
> almost eternal on its branch,
> it was searching for something else.
>
> The rose
> was not searching for darkness or science:
> borderline of flesh and dream,
> it was searching for something else.
>
> The rose
> was not searching for the rose.
> Motionless in the sky
> it was searching for something else.[26]

When I first heard these words of Lorca, two voices rose up in me—a not uncommon experience. The first, soft, fleeting, like a whisper on my lips, said only "yes." The other voice, louder, familiar, insistent, unsatisfied, and nowhere near my lips asked, What is this rose searching for? What is this something else? If the rose is not searching for the light or the darkness or for science or for itself, what can it be searching for? Perhaps if I knew what Lorca was searching for, then I would know what his rose was searching for. What was he projecting into this rose? How is this to be interpreted? How are we to understand it? What does it mean?

Lorca's poem caused this second voice to ask a lot of questions, all sorts of very definite questions, and I could tell right away that if one set out to answer them, one would do so in equally definite ways: intertextually, intratextually, biographically, literarily, psychologically—all the familiar methods and techniques for analyzing, criticizing, interpreting, and explaining a poem and, of course, the poet.

Then I noticed that there were no questions in the poem—only very definite statements. How could Lorca make such definite statements? How does he know the rose was not searching for the sunrise? How does he know that it does not search for science? How does he know it searches at all? How does he know the rose knows something of the borderline between flesh and dream? I noticed I was asking a lot of questions again, wanting to know how he knew, wanting to know what he meant, just wanting to know something. Why couldn't poets say what they mean? Clearly they can't mean what they say!

As I became annoyed and upset with the poem, I could sense in the background, in a not quite expressible form, a feeling that I was doing something "wrong" to the poem and to myself. That night I had this dream:

> I was leafing through Jung's *Memories, Dreams, Reflections* when a piece of paper fell out. On it, poem-like, was written:
> > The poem wants a poem.
> > The dream wants a dream.

Whose "poem" is this? What's it doing in Jung's book? What can it possibly mean that a poem *wants* or that a dream *wants*? And what is the significance of this coupling of a dream and a poem around the same desire: *wanting*?

From somewhere I remembered Beaudelaire's acidic comment that the only proper "criticism" of a work of art was another work of art. This little dream began to feel as if that almost-silent "yes" voice, so readily quashed by all those questions, had risen up in the night, written this little poem, as if it too remembered Beaudelaire's feeling, responding to Lorca's poem with a poem. Quite different from questioning, analyzing, interpreting! And to put it there, right in the middle of Jung's *Memories*, as if to say, "and this too belongs."

This dream has caused me a lot of trouble. My training as a scientist and as an analyst has always oriented me differently to dreams and poems than this dream does. I have learned fairly well how to interpret poems and dreams. I have analyzed poets and dreamers. I can explain what these things mean, and I can teach my students and patients to do the same.

But this dream points to something else. A poem wants a poem; a dream wants a dream, as if a poem's desire is another poem; a dream's desire, another dream. Is this only a figure of speech, a poetic phrase, romantic rhetoric, or worse, metaphoric mush? Or, is something genuine intended, something deeper, actual, real; as if there might be an eros of dreams, an eros of poems, as if a dream or poem itself might embody a seeking, a seeking not for interpretation, criticism, or understanding even, but for *generation*, generation of another poem, another dream, a generative spirit seeking relationship in and through these forms?

I fell into a reverie on Lorca's uncertain borderline of flesh and dream and in my imaginings I experienced a spirited and winged figure leaping across the boundary. This leaping presence startled me. And I felt that strange combination of fright and erotic awakening that accompanies any genuine penetration of consciousness by the unconscious. I fell to wondering what sort of creature this is that leaps across this strange border. Who is this spirit penetrating my reverie with such power? I could only imagine it had something to do with Eros, particularly that sense of Eros that Baynes describes so well in his *Mythology of the Soul*:

> The essential character of Eros is the divine (i.e., the creative) shaft which leaps across the guarded frontier of the subject in order to reach the object. The creative shaft is the impregnating phallus, the impressive, fertilizing image, the creative word, the idea which gets home, the divine leap by which the individual subject is able to transcend his own subjectivity and take an effective part in the work of creation. This is Eros, the god which bringeth twain together in the service of life.[27]

Baynes is describing a spirit that *desires*. And when this spirit penetrates consciousness, the individual is able to transcend the limitations of ego and to take part, not in ego's work, but in the "work of creation," that is, to participate in the birth of the future.

It is this Eros who lies behind this strange little dream: *a dream wants a dream; a poem wants a poem.* In the most astonishing economy of words, this dream says all I would want you to take away from what you are reading here without forgetting. Put this little dream-poem in your pocket. Take it out from time to time and ponder it. This dream was a gift. And in that spirit Lewis Hyde describes so well in *The Gift: The Erotic Imagination and Property*,[28] I want to circulate this dream. Pass it on.

Still, the yearning for that *something else,* like Lorca's rose, perhaps like Rilke's call for "heart-work now,"[29] is not satisfied with just this. The yearning urges speech even as I recognize that this dream almost demands that I speak to you in the language of

dreams, the language of poems, the language of the borderline between flesh and dream. I am acutely aware that ordinary language
fails miserably in this task.

Nevertheless, I have here been helped by one of Jung's late
thoughts written near the end of his life, where he confessed that:

> At this point the fact forces itself on my attention that besides the
> field of reflection there is another equally broad if not broader area
> in which rational understanding and rational modes of representa-
> tion scarcely find anything they are able to grasp. This is the realm
> of Eros. [30]

Clearly, the dream is not a herald of reflection's realm. It is an
arrow of Eros. There is little for reason to grasp. Perhaps trying
"to grasp" is itself the wrong impulse. Dreams do not seek
reason's grasp but seek another kind of touch, a touch I imagine
Lorca's rose would recognize, for it is that touch that is the *something else,* and the kind of touch I imagine there is hunger for in
our time. Dreams and poems spring from some unknown realm
and embody themselves in our experience. They come as *visitors*
seeking something of us. Strangely enough, according to my little
dream, they come seeking dreams and poems in return. What can
this be?

Steel on Stone

I HAVE TAKEN a certain measure of satisfaction in the fact that this is the first in what will become a series of lectures and is "special" simply because it is first. Being first constellates archetypal energies that invariably surround new undertakings. *Undertakings.* I can't go past this word quickly. It has a strange edge to it. I find it difficult to leave words alone when they pull at me this way. I cannot let them run on and do their usual job and perform their usual and useful role of conveying my thoughts in a smooth flow directly to you. It was the poet, Paul Valéry, who observed the subtle irony that "we understand ourselves thanks only to our speed past words."[31]

Speeding past words generates understanding, or at least the illusion of understanding. But the poet asks, perhaps even more than the analyst does: *Is understanding the main thing?* I side with the poet in this and the poet in Jung when he says that "life, at the core, is steel on stone."[32] I want to convince you that understanding without eros leaves one with no way into the world, that the core of eros is *not* understanding, *not* reflection, *not* consciousness, but *enactment:* "steel on stone."

A moment ago, I used the word *undertaking.* Quite unexpectedly, as I was writing along, this word "undertaking" suddenly appeared—just presented itself. And because of this it stands out as if calling to me in some way. I mean this quite literally! In this context, I like Roland Barthes's term, *punctum*,[33] for what attracts his psyche in a photograph, that is, the particular aspect of an image that makes the photograph *exist* for him. The word, like that particularity of the image, also can become suddenly a *punctum*, it "punctures" the smooth flow of conscious intention. Like a dream, a slip of the tongue, a sudden intrusive image, a sudden change in mood, or a momentary forgetting, the flow of ego consciousness is disturbed, disrupted, *punctured!* Rather than "psychopathologies of everyday life," I call these *puncta*, "moments of madness." I see these punctures as eros moments when the unconscious *desires* relationship, moments when psyche as *other* speaks to the ego. To judge these moments as "mistakes," or "pathologies," or "parapraxes" is to miss the call of the other to relationship. These moments should not be treated as failures of the ego. The other in us speaks this way many times a day. I think that most of us, even those well trained to notice, fail these moments when we speed past them in our pursuit of understanding.

I want to emphasize that the *unconscious desires relationship*. I do not experience this as romantic fantasy, as mere figure of speech. Rather, it is that these moments of madness embody the speeches of other figures in us. Not listening becomes a matter of grave concern. Muriel Spark's poem, "Created and Abandoned," provides a haunting sense of what is at issue:

> Where have you gone, how has it ended with you,
> people of my dreams, cut off in mid-life,
>   gone to what grave?
> It's all right for me. I'm fine. I always woke
>   up when we parted
> and saw it was only a dream. I took up my life
> as I left it the day before. How about you?—
> like people with bound feet, or people not
>   properly formed
> without further scope, handicapped. Sometimes
>   I never knew
> what you were going to say, didn't let you speak,
>   but woke.
> You being unreal after all, this means unwell.
>   I worry about you.
> Did something not happen to you after my waking?
> Did something next not happen? Or are you
> limbo'd there where I left you forever,

> like characters
> in a story one has started to write and set aside?
> However bad-mannered you were, however amazing
> in your style, I hope you're not looking for me
> night after night, not waiting for me to come back.
> I feel a definite responsibility for your welfare.
> Are you all right?[34]

Spark's poem envisions a graveyard filled with the forgotten psyche. But, like the "cemetery of dead metaphors"[35] hidden beneath the shell of words, the psychic corpses populating these realms are not dead things. And Spark knows, in spite of her hope, that these forgotten ones are looking for us. Their ghostly presence can be felt even in the sudden appearance of an unexpected word like *undertaking*. Taking this word seriously leads me to see that something is to be taken *under*. And while I speak of a new undertaking and should be in high spirits and ready for celebration, I can't help but notice this strange reminder of death intruding. In the Eros and Psyche tale, death haunts Psyche's every move. It is well to remember that her undertaking in pursuit of Eros took her not only to Hades itself, but to her Stygian sleep as well.

If I were more French, the haunting quality of this undertaking would nonetheless launch me into a reverie on the *pleasure* of the text or *desire* in the act of writing or reading, and before long I would be talking about the erotics of words and how our problems of relationship are so clearly mirrored in our failure to experience and suffer the erotics of language. This sudden appearance of an unexpected word can be one of writing's genuine pleasures, particularly when one is not too rigidly ego-identified with what one intends to write. This vulnerability to the word as unexpected *visitor* is essential to the eros of writing. Writing block is the result of building thick walls to keep eros out! But I am more Scot than French, and my natural reserve prevents me from jumping in so directly. I must go round about.

An Obscene Taming

MY BASIC OPTIMISM is stirred by the idea of undertaking an inauguration of these lectures in spite of a world seemingly bent on destruction, a world so filled with madness. But I quickly despair that anything I could say would have a truly astonishing effect. Of course, I am expecting too much. We get inspired about the adventures of the gods, the sufferings of goddesses, and we take solace and find inspiration in the marvelous similarities of these compelling stories, numinous images, archetypal realities, and our own lives and dreams. And we can be deeply affected and moved and touched. But in three days' time, if not sooner, the gods of everyday life—those powerful yet little-known gods of habit, repetition and "same old story"—these powers swallow it all up and we are left yearning again for another fix of inspiration from dream, from image, from lover, from television, even, in desperation, from lecturer. And in these darker moments we hear echoes of something missing in the everydayness of our life and frequently we sense those things we might have done, those undertakings not taken. It is here we come to know over and over again Dante's frustration with the glacial slowness of social change and how it is mirrored in our slow, sad motions of wanting, of wanting something, of wanting something else.

But more than this. If after reading Jonathan Schell's exposure of the penultimate myth of our time, namely the myth of "murdering the future" through nuclear extermination[36] (the last myth, the eschatological event being its literal enactment), if after going through this excursus on the text of our time—which reveals with almost too much clarity the myth that now shadows all myths, all actions, all realities—if after this one can proceed through one's daily life as before, then something is deeply wrong. Words can be powerful, as we all know. Yet, I fear that words can no longer penetrate deeply enough, that no words are sufficient to the task we face in the world, and for one who loves words and the soul in them this produces a sadness that almost silences me.

But not words only! Images too! Some time ago I watched a television program called "The Wall."[37] It was the story of the Warsaw ghetto in its final days. Before every commercial break, a still shot, frozen on the screen, was presented for a few moments before moving into the string of commercials. I saw there a still picture, not unlike a photograph, of a young child lying face down, murdered there. And, for a moment, the rapid movement of the TV image stopped. I thought in that moment that surely not only is there a speed past words, but a speed past images as well.

Here was this frozen frame, unusual for television, a photograph really, and instantly I experienced what I had found so disturbing yet so compelling in Barthes's book, *Camera Lucida*: "Whether or not the subject is already dead, every photograph is this catastrophe," and how "Society is concerned to tame the photograph, to temper the madness which keeps threatening to explode in the face of whoever looks at it."[38]

Of course, the very movement of television or movie image, and most of the images we experience in our everyday life, keeps us moving always *away* from what we have just seen. In this moving away there is a kind of forgetting. But a photograph rivets us to the spot, forcing us into memory, forcing a movement of psyche. To fix the image, as for example in focusing on the image in a dream, is an eros act that awakens psyche and initiates psyche's movement. We stop this psychic movement only when we move away as in turning away from a photograph or an image or passively letting the images go by us.

As I saw that stopped image on the television screen and was pulled down into its horrible depth, taken under to the reality of Hades on earth, I began to *feel*. I realized deeply: *That has been!* I felt fully what Barthes had been saying, that death lurks in every photograph, realizing too the edge of madness in the invitation to go further into the horror of it, realizing too why we speed past the image and the dream and all those parapraxes of everyday life, speeding so readily into interpretations, analyses, or, as in this instance, into the commercial. We have trouble staying in the stillness, in the silence of not understanding. This frozen image of the dead child was followed by another image, which I could well imagine Barthes calling "an obscene taming." What was it? That woman concerned about seeing her reflection in her dishes? Or was it that man racing another downhill for a beer? Or was it that man leaping into the air with joy about his new car? Or was it that phone ad that said, "wouldn't it be nice if everything worked this well?" Or, maybe it was something about pleasure. I don't remember now. No matter. Suddenly I wanted to abandon all attempts at explanation, all the obscene taming we do in the face of the raw psyche.

What happened in that moment when one image moved into the other was a kind of killing, a murder of feeling. If that's too strong, let's call the succession of such images a psychic violation, a rape of feeling by image. To me, it spoke loudly of the everyday culture we are all both culprits and victims in. But the truly shocking thing about this marriage of horror and banality—a kind of madness we seem to countenance without knowing it—is that one's depth of feeling is led violently into the very worst that materialism has to offer. What is the name of such madness?

The commercial image says: "Yes, children were murdered and slaughtered, still are for that matter, but you can't do anything about it. Don't bother. You can't do anything with that feeling of yours. The real problem, the problem you can do something about is this problem of seeing your reflection in your dishes. If you use this detergent of ours you will be able to see yourself and not only impress your neighbors but your mother as well. Now these things can be done. It's even easy. Just reach for the little bottle the next time you're in the market. Put your money into something you can do something about."

That most of us probably spend more money on dish soap without a second's pause than on alerting our companions to the dangerous myth now enveloping our civilization and all future civilizations is testimony to the effectiveness of subverting deep feeling and human value through the claims and power of money. We need more profound reflection on this coupling of our deepest feeling and money. Feeling loses out. Remember Wally Strawn's plaint in the opening lines of *My Dinner with André*, about how he used to think about music and art, and that now, at age 36, all he thinks about is money. Its funny. But here also is one of the great mythic tragedies of our time for which there may be no future Euripedes to sing its lament. The psyche has trouble expressing itself generatively when the ego is forced to surrender itself to the darker and stronger claims of money.

Even at our Jungian institutes, societies, and foundations—all of them everywhere—the topic of money is at the fore. But only rarely do we hear what the psyche has to say about it. One of our deepest failings as "Jungians," when we gather collectively, is that we leave psyche at the door. We take actions, launch programs, keep up with what we have always done before, all without much inquiry into psyche's views. I am not here talking about some mass group-mindedness, but the eros task of each one of us to bring the reality of the psyche into everything we do. That to me means telling and hearing something beyond the ego. Why not ask for dreams as well as money? Let's see what dreams we gather. Some say that would break the container and lead to psychic infections. Well, I remember that the word for truth comes from the root for tree; I remember a poem that tells of the sadness of those trees in the city, in their little boxes on the street, cut off from the earth that lets them speak to other trees; I remember the trees try to tell passersby that the air they make for us is not such good air when they are cut off from the ground and from other trees; I remember the trees' sadness that passersby will not listen or cannot hear; remembering these things leads me to wonder if we might not need another view of the matter. Romantic, isn't it? Von

Franz says at the end of an interview that "the hope to change the world is a childish illusion. You have to change yourself."[39] Who can doubt it? But once we are changed, as we are changing, I think we must let one another know what psyche is saying. I think we must find ways to do this. If we wonder why our institutes and organizations lose libido, fragment, lose their way, we can find the root problem in not finding ways to hear and listen to psyche's speech. It is only sadder in connection with our organizations because we hoped it would not be so.

It is almost enough to make one agree with André Gregory that everything one hears or reads nowadays contributes to turning you into a robot and that this robot-like state we see every day around us now "...may very well be a self-perpetuating unconscious form of brainwashing created by a world totalitarian government based on money....And that it's not just a question of individual survival...but that somebody who's bored is a-sleep...And somebody who's asleep will not say no."[40] But the scariest thing, particularly if one really listens to the deeper rumblings of dreams, is not some big brother manipulating us behind the scenes. One might take solace from such conspiracy explanations; one can after all seek out and overthrow conspirators. No. The scarier thing and something closer to the reality of the myth we are confronting is that what man has created may be out of his control, that his various monster creations will no longer be available to his command, that the victim in all of this will be the capacity for ultimate choice, a capacity drowned in a frenzied animation of illusory choice that marks our culture today. From choosing a life style to choosing any style there exists a massive seduction of the ego by the concerted power of collective images and a widespread failure of individual choice that would be based on an eros relation of enactment to the call of ones own individual psyche. We are not choosing; we are victims of an endless illusion of choice.

The ego is powerfully subject to imitative influences. This power of mimesis invariably works against one's own individual nature. The psyche always pushes for uniqueness because it is only in bringing uniqueness in relation to other unique natures that relationship is possible at all. Mimesis always keeps one bound in a narcissistic failure to develop uniquely. This, I believe, is why Jung wrote to Aniela Jaffé and said: "I must confess I was against the C. G. Jung Institute only from aversion to the prominence given to my name. However, that can be changed."[41] As far as I can see no institute, foundation, society, or group has changed its name. The name of Jung is carried into the name of what we do at every turn. Even here we continue this tradition by inaugurating the C. G. Jung Lectures. Why was Jung averse? And on what ground do we go against his feeling in attaching his name to our activities and to ourselves? What would we call ourselves if we did not use his name?

I once had a dream in which I was walking along a path with Jung. We were holding hands. We were in deep discussion. Suddenly, we came to a point where there were many branching paths. He said to me: "We have walked together as far as we can. We now go our separate ways." That is what Jung's psychology calls us to. His psychology can take us to our own path. Then we must go our own way. Mimesis at that point is the very opposite and bedevils much of what we do. We don't have a proper noun for what Jung did so we use his name. We can't call it psychotherapy; we can't call it analysis; we can't call it analytical psychology. We do call it these things, and we have unsettled arguments about whether what we do is "Jungian." Of such things Jung said: "The clinical practice of psychotherapy is a mere makeshift that does its utmost to prevent numinous experience."[42]

Jung loved the psyche. We don't have a noun for that because it's a verb. We don't have a language of verbs. Our psychological language weakens itself by insisting on the primacy of nouns and adjectives and working to weaken verbs. "That is shadow." "That woman in your dreams is anima." "That is projection." Nouns and adjectives work for distance, keeping the ego in a superior position of naming and hence having power over, standing over, the objects of our experience. It is the language of subject and object distinctions: pointing at. Verbs relativize the ego, immersing it in something else: "He shadows you," "she animates you," "it projects you." Verb language takes the *is* out of the superior position, emphasizing not the existence of things, but the *relationship* between things. Writing and language of this form is very alive because transitive verbs bring eros. Shakespeare's writing is erotic through his use of vivid verbs and casting out "is" constructions. Even the writing of microphysics is animated because in that realm only relationships exist—not separate objects. The subject-object vantage point disappears. Psyche becomes one with matter. This eventually will require a new language of us, and it will be an eros language of relationship.

If we are what we speak, we will see that our current psychological language concerns itself with reflection's nouns and adjectives. The verbs of eros are missing. It seems to me that women are carrying most of the burden of verbs in our time while men are still identified with nouns and adjectives. And so it was in that television movie, when in the face of annihilation the men wanted to form a committee to reflect on the matter. It was a woman's voice that spoke out for the deeper necessity of acting. That necessity is the realm of eros, that realm, as Jung said, "in which rational understanding and rational modes of representation scarcely find anything they are able to grasp."[43] While reflection generates understanding through withdrawal of projection's energy from the world and aims toward differentiation and separation, eros generates activity in the world through connection and immersion in and with "the other." Both are essential. Both are necessary. But it is eros that needs emphasis now because among us reflection too often prevents it, undermining the capacity and the confidence and the courage to deal with the consequences of what we do. Too often we are left reflecting on life rather than living it.

Even as long ago as 1930, Freud saw the importance of Eros in the coming time:

> The fateful question of the human species seems to me to be whether and to what extent the cultural process developed in it will succeed in mastering the derangements of communal life by the human instinct of aggression and self destruction. In this connection, perhaps the phase through which we are at this moment passing deserves special interest. Men have brought their powers of subduing the forces of nature to such a pitch that by using them they could now very easily exterminate one another to the last man. They know this—hence arises a great part of their current unrest,

their dejection, their mood of apprehension. And now it may be expected that the other of the two *heavenly forces*, eternal Eros, will put forth his strength so as to maintain himself alongside of his equally immortal adversary.[44]

Freud's call for the advent of Eros is an insight (or prayer!) of enormous proportions. I'm not sure anyone heard him. Perhaps it was because Freud seems to be speaking from the vantage point of an objective observer of the human species, as if from outer space. It may follow from the same condition that allowed him to say two years later that "our best hope for the future is that the intellect—the scientific spirit, reason—should in time establish a dictatorship over the human mind. Whatever...opposes such a development is a danger for the future of mankind."[45] Here Freud seems to forget his call to Eros and falls into the typical stance of siding with reason against the soul. I feel Freud's earlier sense was more correct, that the battle is not between Eros and Logos but between Eros and Thanatos. Thanatos seems ever-present in today's world. But where is Eros?

These two themes are related. It is a certainty that with the advent of the means of extermination of all life as we know it, an unholy alliance has grown up between the rational intellect and this final power, this incarnation of Thanatos. With this supreme achievement of the patriarchal mind—which we might think of as burning the wings of eros with too much light—Eros must flee, must refuse to take up the battle in so much light, must seek, first, a nursing elsewhere. Can a god be wounded by what man does? If "...it is we who will save God," in the words of Kazantzakis,[46] if "God can be made conscious," as Jung argues throughout *Answer to Job*,[47] then surely "gods can be wounded" by what we do. After all, if the gods are dead, who was it that killed them?

If we take Jung's idea that even God needs the help of man's consciousness to become more fully conscious, to see this consciousness as necessary for the incarnation of the spirit, then we might enlarge this whole idea and say that Eros too needs our consciousness (perhaps even more, our eros, our love), if that "father-mother of all higher consciousness"[48] is to incarnate ever more fully in our life, in our time.

But how do we accomplish this in any practical sense? Jung says it most clearly in what I consider to be his most crucial letter, a letter written in 1960, to Sir Herbert Read:

We have simply got to listen to what the psyche spontaneously says to us. What the dream, which is not manufactured by us, says is *just so*....It is the great dream which has always spoken through the artist as a mouthpiece. All his love and passion (his "values") flow towards the coming guest to proclaim his arrival....What is the great Dream? It consists of the many small dreams and the many acts of humility and submission to their hints. It is the future and the picture of the new world, which we do not understand yet. We cannot know better than the unconscious and its intimations. *There* is a fair chance of finding what we seek in vain in our conscious world. Where else could it be?[49]

On Market Street

I WOKE UP WITH TEARS in my eyes saying the last line of a poem I was telling to an unknown audience. I was actually saying the line as I woke up and the line was: *where madness is psyche's only nurse.* The audience was tearful. I was tearful. I had never experienced such congruence, such absolute interpenetration of dream and waking world. I immediately fell into a mood of anguish over the image of psyche in need of nurse, realizing how much more readily, even still, I nurse ego instead. And then the threat: was it to be madness, then, that would nurse psyche in me?

Was it like that time not so long ago after a gathering of my colleagues—at which we all participated in a brutalization of psyche—when I walked out into the middle of the night, asleep, walked into the woods seeing trees full of women's faces with tears flowing in a great flood, hearing the air filled with lamenting cries, and a wailing voice commanding me to follow that river of tears to where it met the sea; and, in doing this, finally awakening, finding myself kneeling on the sand, with water in my hands, wondering whether I *might* have walked straight into the sea? And feeling, after remembering this now, that no, it's not women only who are suffering in our time, not even the feminine only; psyche is victim, psyche itself in need of nursing.

And I thought that madness must nourish psyche because in

our enormous capacity to deny the imaginative reality that is psyche, to reserve reality only to the material world we call reality, that denied and rejected psyche will in fact become *matter* before our eyes. Who can deny the reality of psyche when one walks our streets today? It is visible, present, materialized in the behavior and bodies and the voices we try not to see, try not to hear. Psyche has become real in this way because we fail in so many ways to grant psyche reality. If we can't find food for psyche, psyche will feed on madness, nurse on madness.

But what was I doing in the guise of a poet? It was clearly "my" poem I was telling. Yet, I lay no claim to be a poet. And who was this unknown audience? Who was it that was hearing me and being so affected? And here again I felt that curious mixture of poem and dream together. What does it mean? Well, I had already learned my lesson about too many questions. Besides, it was time to go teach my seminar that day in San Francisco, a seminar I had called "Psyche into Words."

The workshop went very well and I was quite "high"—a California colloquialism for inflation. Afterward, I went walking along Market Street. It's something I like to do in cities: walk along a main street so I can feel the pulse and soul of the city. One end of Market Street is the high style of the financial district; the other is the haunt of "the crazies," as they are known. That day, as I walked, the line from my dream kept haunting me. I had asked everyone in the seminar to write a poem that night, and, of course, I would have to do so as well. I kept trying to recapture something of the rest of the dream poem, but without any success. Then suddenly, right there on Market Street, a quick series of unexpected events occurred and I sat down on the sidewalk, back against a building, in the habitat of the crazies, writing as fast as I could something that was reeling itself off from somewhere in the interior. It was not my voice but it was speaking as if it were me. The words were absolutely clear and I wrote down what the psyche was *spontaneously* saying and writing it on the only paper I had—a MasterCard receipt. Here is what I heard on Market Street:

I walked Market Street today
    you know that place
    junk stores
    and some say
    junk people
where I tried on that Greek fisherman's cap
    authentic
    at 10.99
    my head was too big
    my head was too big
    my head is too big
became a chorus right there on Market Street
    but no one heard
    except this guy who
    shot out of that store
    like an unguided missile
    whose any target will do
    meant me
and this junked man he crashed into me
    and when I said sorry
    like mama taught me to do
    in all special circumstances
    he only said
    in a commander's voice supreme
    at ease
and in the very next breath was shocked
    into recognition
    of who was soldier
    and who was commander
    exactly
and that junked man commander saluted
    my head too big
    and shouted with respect in-boned
    yes sir
    yes sir
    and I knew that
from analyst to commander on Market Street
    is not an easy promotion
    yet I took his gift of rank
    and its cap just right
    when I heard him shout
    at ease
    and saw him salute
    and yes sir
    yes sir

> even to that girl with one arm
>   that girl not even bumped into
>   became a commander too
>   on Market Street
> today when girls are commanders
>   who will be nurses
>   who will be nurses
>   on Market Street
>   when that man
>   that mad man
> has made commanders of us all
>   it will be yes
>   it will be madness
>   yes madness itself yes
>   because on Market Street
>   where I walked today
>   is where madness is psyche's only nurse.

I didn't compose these lines in any way that I can claim them, in the same sense that I cannot claim to have composed the dream. In this sense it can only be ego's hubris to claim a dream or such a poem as "mine." But I was there. I was witness. The dream was a visitor, these events visitors, and they formed themselves into what seems like a poem. It was almost as if these realities wanted to become a poem. As if such a poem is another kind of dream. But most certainly the psyche wanted these events remembered and spoken out in this way. Psyche wanted this to be heard. I began to feel that the dream, those events, and the poem were the beginnings of an answer to some question I had not yet asked but which was beginning to stir in me.

Of course, we can all interpret the poem and even its poet. Even so, the fate of all interpretations is to remain *about*. "Not ideas about the thing but the thing itself,"[50] says Wallace Stevens—a lesson we have yet to learn in psychology. Yet, if the poem or dream can stay for a time before being taken too quickly to understanding's realm, then in the ear, or in the night, or on the street, we may hope to hear not what ego has to say, but what psyche has to say in response. Can one trust that a poem wants a poem, a dream wants a dream? I think so. I hope to show that in this trust lies a fundamental secret of Eros.

PART TWO

Innocent Ears and Willing Tongues

There is a land of the living and a land of the dead and the
bridge is love, the only survival, the only meaning.

—*Thornton Wilder*

"Inaugurating's" Hidden Image

IN CHINESE UNIVERSITIES, *pi i niao* means "metaphor." In the streets of the city, the word is used for "friend." In the fields, the peasants, not quite remembering why, say *pi i niao* when they want to speak of "man and wife." Hidden in the word's forgotten history is the image of a fabulous bird with one wing who needed a mate in order to fly. He found his one-winged mate, and folding together with her, became the legendary great bird *pi i niao*, image of deepest union. The more sophisticated we become the more distant we are from the images hidden in the language we use. Just as we lose contact with the earth when our hands reach for plastic and tin at the supermarket instead of the dirt and living things of the ground, we lose contact with the living earth of our language when we become separated from those concrete images hidden in our words.

I once heard a voice in a dream that asked me: "Do you not know that words are eggs, that words carry life, that words give birth?" At that time I didn't. But I felt the dream to be a task, took the hint, and by acting on it, my relation to words has changed. I have come to know in a better way what Jung meant when he said that "our words carry the totality of that history which was once so alive and still exists in every human being."[51] *Still exists in every human being!* How little we know this! How little we connect to it! Bachelard knew it: "for a word dreamer there are words which

43

are *shells of speech (coquilles de parole)*. Yes, by listening to certain words as a child listens to the sea in a seashell, a word dreamer hears the murmur of a world of dreams *(songes)*."[52]

Listening at the shell of a word is accomplished first by a kind of etymological reverie, a kind of playing in the word's roots, nestings and branchings, playing with the old word meanings that "still reverberate in the unconscious chambers of the soul."[53] By slowing down, listening, playing with the word, one begins to hear what the word is saying. It is not without considerable significance that Jung said a dream could not possibly be understood unless one does this:

> Our actual mind is the result of the work of thousands or perhaps a million years. There is a long history in every sentence, every word we speak has a tremendous history, every metaphor is full of historical symbolism; they would not carry at all if that were not true. Our words carry the totality of that history which was once so alive and still exists in every human being. With every word we touch upon a historical fibre, as it were, in our fellow beings; and therefore every word we speak strikes that chord in every other living being whenever we speak the same language....
>
> So we can't possibly understand a dream if we don't understand the atmosphere, the history of the underlying images. There are personal problems in dreams which one may think only important for that particular case, but if one goes deeply enough into the structure, the speech symbolism, one enters historical layers and discovers that what seemed to be merely a personal problem goes much deeper, it reaches the analyst himself and everybody who hears it. One can't help bringing in the way in which our ancestors tried to express the same problem, and that leads one to historical matter....
>
> ...It all comes out of the same unconscious mind, the irrational and eternal stock, the pre-functioning collective unconscious, which repeats itself throughout the centuries, a sort of eternal, imperishable language.[54]

So if I was to inaugurate the C. G. Jung Lectures, I at least ought to know what the word *inaugurate* carries as its secret and hidden image.

If I tell you a contemporary dictionary definition, what you will experience is a triumph of the modern rational mind, an achievement of that impulse which is part of our contemporary problem. As you can tell immediately, a definition like "to begin officially," leaves one bored, unmoved. Psyche is not stirred. Hence the robot quality of much of our language. The computer will save us a lot of time here because it can do this sort of thing better and faster than any human can. Certainly in this way of speech there is no reverberation in those unconscious chambers of the soul, no murmur of dreams, no hint of deep history, no sense of eggs carrying life. We do feel that we understand something by this turning words into other words in a circular fashion and we are assisted in this understanding by that ever seductive instantaneous speed past the word. Yet there is nothing in that definition that would keep us lingering at the word, as we might at a deep well, looking down, where we might, with the poet Jimenez, begin to quiver and sense that it is "the word itself that pierces, gyrating, the dark earth until it reaches the cold water,"[55] and the dryness of the speeding mouth is quenched. A way with words that would experience them as wells! We might then understand what Jimenez tells Platero, his donkey: "Platero, if one day I throw myself into this well, it will not be, believe me, to kill myself, but to catch the stars more quickly."[56]

We do not linger at the word because, just like a dream image, we are curious more often only for meaning. Valéry says:

> You have certainly observed the curious fact that a given *word* which is perfectly clear when you hear it or use it in *everyday* language, and which does not give rise to any difficulty when it is engaged in the rapid movement of an ordinary sentence becomes magically embarrassing, introduces a strange resistance, frustrates any effort at definition as soon as you take it out of circulation to examine it separately and look for its meaning after taking away its instantaneous function.[57]

So we hurry into meanings. We have difficulty staying in a state of *not knowing*, a state that is essential to reverie. Not knowing is an eros moment, and if we linger there psyche begins to speak spontaneously. But as with a well, to see the stars, eyes must adjust to darkness; so, too, ears must adjust to silence. We do not linger at the word because death is there. Whenever we don't know, the great unknown intrudes ever so slightly, and the great unknown is death. That's why every dream brings with it a bit of death. We don't need to take the dream to the underworld. That great unknown is brought to us. That is the secret power of the symbol, that is, in Jung's sense of symbol as "something that still belongs entirely to the domain of the unknown or something that is yet to be."[58] What is not fully known, of course, is that the future and the major content of the future for each of us is death. The symbols that are most "alive" to us paradoxically concern this great unknown.

It is useful then to turn to what is "dead" in language, to rummage about in the "cemetery of dead metaphor," in order to resurrect the ghosts that are yet alive in our words. We have completely lost our sense of the word as *museum,* forgetting that museum means not only the place of dead things, but the place of the Muses, and by forgetting, *forgetting* this most essential bit of mythology, we deny the Muses a place in our sense of the word. And when we forget this deeply, we no longer experience what Emerson experienced when he said that "every word was once a poem"[59] and because of this we no longer know what poetry is for, or how to hear it, or how to make it.

To remember "inaugurate" requires going into the cemetery of this word, to turn to what is "dead" (the dead languages) in pursuit of the hidden image as a way of enlivening the word. Our English word "inaugurate" rises up out of the Old Latin word *inauguro,* literally, "to take omens from the flight of birds." You see how quickly one is on different ground! Even the "official" meanings of the old language seem imaginal to us. The reason is that the definition is an image of a literal act and at its root is an active verb. And *inauguro*? From the Latin *augur,* that is, "soothsayer": a teller of sooth. Not a teller of soothing, but of sooth, that is, "things of truth and reality." Soothsayer. Omens. Birds. Now you begin to experience what is hidden in this inaugurating.

There is more hidden history in this word that will be useful to hear. In early Rome, there were two great categories of priests: the *Pontifices* and the *Augures.* Those who were members of the *Colleguim Pontificum* would issue pronouncements, proclamations, interpretations, and explanations, and otherwise carry out the official duties of the state religion. Our word "pontificate" in its full range of meanings relates to this order with its emphasis on authority, dogma, tradition, orthodoxy. All religions, organizations, and institutions of whatever sort have a "collegium pontificum." At one time or another, perhaps quite a lot of the time, each of us wears the robes of this order. Sometimes we can't take them off.

Those who were members of the *Collegium Augurium* had the specific task of making known the future by observing the heavens, the flights, calls, and behavior of birds, visions, and dreams, the appearance of various animals, and any unusual occurrences, the latter being of the type we would now call synchronistic events. The *Augures* would observe things carefully, whether met with accidentally or specifically watched for. They were to make known to those in power whether the gods approved of whatever was planned or about to be set in motion. The *Augures* could only advise. They lacked power.

The priestly *Augures* were founded by Numa, second king of Rome, who also instituted the worship of Vesta and established the guardians of Vesta's fire, the Vestal Virgins. He was guided in this inaugurating by Tacita, one of the Muses, or Muta as she was sometimes called. She was the goddess of silence—may still be. As I pull these bits of thread together, I feel a rising excitement as I think now of that little entrance to the inner ear, that anatomical place called the vestibule, or, literally, the "habitat of Vesta." Vesta's name derives from a root meaning "to dwell," "to stay the night," and with derivatives meaning "to be." No one ever discovered the secret of the Vestal Virgins. But the image of the word dwelling in the ear, spending the night, invites erotic meditation, invites it because it concerns what is inexpressible, and that is the essence of eros, that "something else." It's the beginning of innocent ears. This sensuous texture of language is within reach. Imagine playing this way with the "mother tongue." Can one suppress the image of playing with mother's tongue, that object which plays such a crucial role in speech, that object which so excited your curiosity when you were a child?

Listen to Rilke:

> It was a girl, really—there is a double joy
> of poetry and music that she came from—

> and I could see her glowing through her spring clothes:
> she made a place to sleep inside my ear.
>
> And she slept in me. Her sleep was everything.
> The trees I'd always loved, those distances that we
> can almost touch, the pastures I felt so much,
> and every miracle I found in myself.
>
> She was sleeping it all. Wild Singing God,
> how did you do it so that she had no desire at all
> to be awake? See, she got up sleeping.
>
> And when will she die? And you want to find this out,
> also even before your poem fades?
> Where is she going to, as she sinks away... a girl really...[60]

The *Augures* were born out of the inspiration of silence and that is why they were watchers, seers, hearers, listeners, observers. They weren't talking all the time like the *Pontifices!* The *Augures* carried not the long, straight, and so obviously phallic staff of the *Pontifices,* but the *lituus,* the curiously crooked, curving, spiraling staff that so readily reminds one of the spiraling cochlea and those semicircular canals, which we call the labyrinth of the inner ear. The *Pontifices* spoke out with their full power and weight and with the full authority and dogma of their religion. The *Augures* spoke in quiet whispers of the signs they saw and heard in their strange and weird experiences all those irrational and subtle moments when one feels the portent of the uncertain and unknown future. To inaugurate, then, is to attend and care for the old echoes of still-living breath but unheeded psyche in this word; to speak as augur, with silence as muse. Such is the sense of this word's voice in my ear.

Enacting the Dream's Hint

NOW TO ECHO back some of the thoughts embedded in that crucial letter Jung wrote to Herbert Read in September 1960. In a tone of urgency, Jung speaks of the necessity to listen to the spontaneous psyche. What the dream says is "just so" and is not "manufactured" by us. In this sense the dream is not "ours" and the ego cannot justifiably claim any achievement. Speaking of "my" dream is a kind of hubris, something like claiming that a tree is "mine" because it's on my property. The dream, like the tree, is nature's speech. The dream is manufactured by "something else" and that "something else" is speaking autonomously and we must, Jung says, listen to this spontaneous speech. He argues that this speaking is linked to a "great dream," a dream that chooses the *artist* as mouthpiece for psyche's speech. It is the artist, perhaps more exactly the "artist's soul," that we must listen to. Jung speaks here of the artist's value as flowing out in love and passion—which we could truly call the eros of the artist's soul—this eros flows "outward" to proclaim the arrival of the coming guest. *The coming guest!* The approaching guest awakens and arouses the welcoming eros of the artist. This points to *art* as carrying the special and vital function of announcing and proclaiming the arrival of the coming guest. I would imagine Jung did not mean mimetic art, ego-based art, nor collective-engendered art, but art that finds its origin in the spontaneous psyche, in that ground of "the other" in us. And it is not the other as shadow but the other as the beginning sparks of an emerging dominant in the objective psyche. Individually, it would be *acts* of art, living expressions of the spontaneous psyche, that provide the welcoming spirit for the coming guest. Jung's letter points to an intimate relationship between act, eros and art. Klee too spoke of this when he said: "My hand is entirely the instrument of a more distant sphere. Nor is it my head that functions in my work; it is something else."[61]

The "great Dream"[62] of which Jung speaks is not only "the secretly perceived made visible"[63] through the hands, words, or acts of the artist, but "consists of the many small dreams" and, most crucially, "the many acts of humility and submission" to the dream's hint. The "great Dream" is born from following, submitting to, humbling oneself and one's ego to the hint of the dream: *to act on the hint of the dream.* An eros relation to the dream must lie in enacting the dream's hint. Of course, Jung insists that the ego must be in a state whereby it can choose consciously to do this. In this lies "the future and the picture of the new world." Jung says we do not understand it yet.

I believe the eros of enactment generates meaning through doing and the consequences of doing, not through ideas of doing or mere understanding of images. It is not a matter of knowledge or even of consciousness: "we cannot know better than the unconscious and its intimations." It is in the unconscious, in that source of psyche's speech, that we may find what is lost to us in the conscious world. It is there that we will find that "something else."

I want to follow the path of the most compelling *punctum* in Jung's letter: the image of the "coming guest." Who is this strange guest at the door? Who is this figure knocking at our door so portentiously? And what is portended? And why is it the artist's love and passion, the artist's eros, that when it flows towards the coming guest will proclaim and welcome this awe-inspiring arrival? Is it art that opens the door? Is this guest invited, or is this appearance unbidden? And why such *personification*? So many questions!

The Coming Guest

THE GREAT PROBLEM of our time is that we don't understand what is happening to the world. We are confronted with the darkness of the soul, the unconscious. It sends up its dark and unrecognizable urges. It hollows out and hacks up the shapes of our culture and its historical dominants. We have no dominants any more, they are in the future. Our values are shifting, everything loses its certainty, even *sanctissima causalitas* has descended from the throne of the *axioma* and has become a mere field of probability. Who is the awe-inspiring guest who knocks at our door so portentiously?[64]

Written near the end of his life, these words of Jung's clearly show he was sensing a new dominant arising from the chaos of a world losing its way. To have no dominants is a chaos where everything has equal claim. So, we might frame our basic question not so much as what is the new development in Jungian psychology, but what does Jungian psychology know of this approaching guest? How is Jungian psychology expressing its love and passion and value in welcoming this guest? And what does Jungian psychology know of the *art* that speaks to this? These questions are not for some distant "Jungian psychology," some institution located somewhere far away. These are questions facing each of us individually, each of our communities, each of our institutions.

Jung is speaking of the future—auguring really—and speaking

with great passion. Almost by necessity, interpretation and analysis of psyche are oriented toward the past. In our psychology, this takes the form of a predilection to refer images backward to prior cultural images: Greek gods, Sumerian goddesses, Latin divinities. There is nothing wrong in this. I love to do it myself. But we ought to notice that what we are calling upon from past people are the products of their imaginative and spontaneous psyche: their poems, their songs, their stories, their sculptings, their ritual drama, in short, we call upon the *art* of prior time, the wealth of story and picture of past ages. And, without question, the modern ego, bereft as it is of much that is genuinely nurturing, finds comfort and solace as well as hope and courage in these previous forms and expressions as they are analogously re-enacted in our present experience. Our archetypal perspective and commitment to the timeless and eternal images of the soul support this work.

But my concern is this: that in our eager pursuit of past mythological images, we may miss relating to the actual myth-inducing, myth-producing quality of the psyche in our own time. The psyche has not abandoned its mythic capacity, its mythic generation, its mythic speech. Myth is not something that happened long ago and is now only repeating, remembered, re-told, or re-presented. Myth is not written once and for all as if to render all future psyches mimetic to stories already told. Myth is speech of the psyche at any time, and it may even be more crucial to be conscious and involved in the mythic voice of the present and future than of the past. I believe it may not be as crucial to consciously "re-vision" or "re-voice" what has been as to become consciously involved and committed to experiencing directly the voices and visions of the spontaneous psyche in our time.

What is meant by the "spontaneous" psyche? It is time to slow down and listen to this word. What images are hidden here? It rises most directly from the Latin *sponte*, meaning "of its own accord" and, in our present context, we can think of this as arising from the intention of something other than the conscious ego. The root of "spontaneous" is *spen-*, which means "to draw across," "to stretch," "to spin." This root gives rise as well to our word *spider*.

One begins to sense a "web" in this word. This is exactly the texture of the word that is so missing when we pass by the word too quickly. You just can't get to the image of a spider weaving a web when you think of "spontaneous" any other way than through this etymological excursion or through dreams. Dreams seem to "remember" these connections, and some of the seemingly strange connections between images in a dream are etymological roots made visible, which in our unknowing, seem inexplicable. This is why Jung said we need to know the etymology of the dream images if we are to get a proper connection to the dream. So too in the word "spontaneous." It is as if something is "thrown across" to us, spanning the gap between conscious and unconscious, thrown across of its own accord, a web of entanglement. There is a web and a spider in any spontaneous speech of the psyche. No wonder one resists so readily! There is also something else. Born of this root is the Greek word *penia*, meaning "lack" and "poverty," an important thing to know because Penia was one of the mythic mothers of Eros. If you sense something of the spinning of the Fates in the background of this you are correct. In this sense, what comes spontaneously from the psyche has a great deal to do with our fate.

To conform what is now moving in the depths of the psyche to forms that have been before may fail the task that lies before each of us. New mythologies rarely develop out of continuations or re-enactments of what has been before. Even the old gods and goddesses wanted to participate and be celebrated in new life! Clearly, Jung is implying that the unconscious is speaking about the world directly—not only about the individual psyche. He says, "we don't understand what is happening to the world." He is also emphasizing that these images are unrecognizable as if to suggest that our usual ways of comprehending and grasping an image are not sufficient to the task. For Jung to speak of not "recognizing" the images being cast up from the unconscious is a monumental statement, for he was rarely lacking in ideas or language about an image from a dream. His wealth of experience and vast background in the images of numerous cultures were always sufficient to resonate with any image presented. There is only one exception:

It is in that case where Jung says that reason finds nothing to grasp onto, where even language fails. It is inarticulateness in the face of Eros. Words won't do because *acts* are required in relation to Eros. The unrecognizability and the futurity that Jung emphasizes, coupled with Freud's call for the appearance of that second great heavenly power, begins to point to Eros as the coming guest. But is it the Eros we know in our mythologies?

To generalize an image's uniqueness in spontaneous expressions of the psyche to already-known mythic patterns will be experienced as a kind of security by ego consciousness. This is an essential step in connecting the ego to its mythological origins and the working ground on which the healing power of these mythical images work. But in the same way that we often tend to overlook the intimate details of a mythic story by pulling out only a thread or two from an exceedingly interwoven fabric, we likewise overlook many of the details of imagery that are "unrecognizable" in the pattern and unique in their quality. Often we are more attracted to the details of imagery that can be readily comprehended, referred to known aspects of a known context, where we can quickly rush into a kind of settledness. What gets overlooked and quickly forgotten is the fine and subtle detail that is unique—absolutely unique. Yet one's exact fate and individuality are tied to those details. Not just the tree as oak, but the angle of the branches, their thickness, their color and much more is in that acorn. The unknown and unrecognized details that are not readily comprehended or understood must not be forgotten. What is more to the point is to be silent in the face of them and let *them* speak.

In order to find ways to tolerate the unrecognized in psyche's spontaneous productions we must be silent and forget in a rather special ways. You will recall Jung's frequent statement to learn all you can and then forget it and face the dream afresh with open eyes and open ears rather than trying to turn the dream's images into speeches you've already heard. Since there always seems to be much more anxiety about not "knowing enough" and very little anxiety about "forgetting enough," I assume that very few if any of us practice what Jung was suggesting. Of course to practice this would require not so much an act of will—you can't forget something if someone asks you to deliberately forget it—but some kind of ritual. One's own individual approach to ritually listening to a dream—one's own or another's—is exceedingly critical. But we don't know too much about it.

Older rituals do provide a hint as to how we might begin to appreciate the necessity of ritual listening. In approaching a healing temple, for example, after a fast, it was common to put an initiate through certain experiences designed to eliminate conscious concerns. In Greek rituals, this was accomplished by drinking a bit of water from the river Lethe—"The River of Forgetting." This was to clear the mind of what we would now call "ego concerns." Next, the initiate was given water from the river Mnemosyne—"The River of Remembering," this for the purpose of remembering not the past but the future, that is, what the initiate would experience in the inner chambers during the secret parts of the ceremony. In this way, as initiates underwent the secret experience, their minds would be alive not with ego concerns but with a readiness to take in and remember the spontaneous and numinous events they would encounter in the depths of the temple.

In this regard it would seem our forgetting of dreams would be the result of using the waters of Lethe to forget too well the spontaneous psyche. Here it is well to remember that Mnemosyne was the mother of the Muses, so that if we understand this correctly, Mnemosyne would give birth to spontaneous impulses toward speech, song, art, dance, poetry, and other manifestations rendering the numinous visible and experiential—not just spoken of and about, but *enacted*. But not only for ourselves! For the numinous, coming as a spark from the objective psyche concerns everyone. We must each become tellers and doers in relation to what we experience there. This is the new development we are searching for. How little we know that the work we do in this is critical to everyone and to the world.

If we lose connection to the living blood of the psyche, we will not only find ourselves in an "endless retailing of accumulated knowledge,"[65] but we will come to know that state so devastatingly pictured by Orozco in his Dartmouth murals—that image of the "gods of the modern world" in academic costume, with the background showing the world in flames, and in the foreground, still-born knowledge being delivered as a birth from a skeleton lying upon a bed of books. "Dead things giving birth to dead things."[66] We could interpret this painting in light of our psychological knowledge. But what if we reverse this and say that the artist has given us a vision of the "gods of the modern world." Here is a contemporary myth right before our eyes. Let's take it as the "just so" Jung speaks of in connection with the dream. Then we would have to look at our psychology and our institutions in the light of these images and take them to heart. Where do we do this? Where are we victims of this world Orozco pictures? Where are we giving birth to dead things while the world is aflame? How are we prisoners of the book?[67] How are we not realizing that the psyche is the best library because it is alive with what has been (the Song of Memory) and pregnant with the future (the Song of the Muses)?

"Interpretation's" Hidden Image

I
N A FOOTNOTE concerning the "coming guest," Adler describes how Jung encountered a "parallel figure" in a book called *The Candle of Vision: The Autobiography of a Mystic*, by the Irish poet George William Russell, otherwise known by the initials, AE.[68] Adler says the book had a profound effect on Jung. Russell, along with Yeats, was a driving force in the Irish literary renaissance in the late nineteenth and early twentieth centuries. In the judgment of Leslie Shepard, *The Candle of Vision*, first published in 1920, "is one of the most important records of the mystic life ever written."[69] There is little reason to argue with this assessment. In spite of the profound effect this book had on Jung, AE was never mentioned in Jung's published works or letters. AE had called the figure Jung encountered in reading *The Candle of Vision*, "the Pilgrim of Eternity." It is not known when Jung first encountered it. This is not the place to go into AE's work at any length, but because he is absent from the literature of analytical psychology, a brief sampling of his writing is necessary. *The Candle of Vision* describes AE's direct experience with the spontaneous psyche before the turn of the century. He writes:

> By the time I was seventeen or eighteen my brain began to flicker with vivid images. I tried to paint these....Something ancient and eternal seemed to breathe through my fancies....I asked myself what legend I would write under the picture. Something beyond reason

57

> held me, and I felt like one who is in a dark room and hears the breathing of another creature, and himself waits breathless for its utterance, and I struggled to understand what wished to be said, and at last...and intent, something whispered to me, "Call it the birth of Aeon."[70]

At the time of this experience (some time in 1884), when AE[1]'s brain began "to flicker" with such spontaneous imagery, AE knew nothing of mystical ideas, nothing of literature, nothing that would have entered directly into his experience as knowledge of "Aeon." Even so, he was compelled to paint these images. He stayed in the presence of "the other," beyond reason, and waited for it to speak. And it spoke. And as often happens when one listens as deeply as AE did to this "other" in him, the experience opens up to synchronistic phenomena that "point the way." Such was AE's experience. A fortnight after hearing that whispering voice say "Call it the birth of Aeon," while in a Library checking out an art book, his eye fell upon a dictionary of religions by chance lying open upon the counter and there on the page leaping out to him was the name Aeon! And there he discovered the Gnostic Aeon, the first created being, the Aeon that true to his own imaginal experience "revolted against heaven and left its courts, descending into the depths where it mirrored itself in chaos, weaving out of the wild elements a mansion for its spirit. That mansion was our earth and that Aeon was the God of our world."[71]

As one reads *The Candle of Vision* closely, one becomes aware of all the basic and crucial ideas and methods we find in Jung. I would imagine it was not only the image of the "Eternal Pilgrim" that impressed Jung, but the entire book, and perhaps not the least being that this was a poet! It has been said often enough that Freud's discovery was nothing that artists had not already known, and it is clear in the early papers on the method of free association that what was in fact shown in free association was the essence of the artist's method, that is, a silencing of the ego to let the psyche speak.[72] But Jung's relation to art and artists was a much more difficult one. As much as Jung encouraged the expression of the images of the unconscious as he had done himself, he was often suspicious of the artist *as* artist. His articles on Picasso and Joyce exhibit this, and his numerous attacks on modern art are well known. Jung had even walked out on Herbert Read's Eranos lecture in which Read defended modern art, had taken Jung to task for his too-narrow view of modern art and the modern artist. Their relationship was nearly ruptured. Jung was suspicious that the modern artist's art was a substitute for life and that the artist was not conscious of what he was doing and for that reason no ethical consequences followed from the artist's creations. I do not believe AE is subject to this criticism.

I believe that Jung's early view of the artist has had rather sad consequences for our psychology. Art's value is sought primarily as a kind of therapy or, if not ignored entirely, art is treated as something to be *analyzed* for its symbolic content, and this usually amounts to illustrating how the work of art can be interpreted and and understood in our psychology and how the work of art provides further evidence for the correctness of our views.[73]

But if Jung's later intuition of "the coming guest" and its relation to art is correct, the task of our time is not to produce interpretations of art nor to cut psychology off from artistic and aesthetic value. The task seems to me to be for anyone who has a sense of the reality of the psyche, to give birth to, to inaugurate, to bring into reality, into literal manifestation, those "urges," those "promptings," those "hints" that in their proclaiming will serve as welcome to the coming guest.

I have been unkind to *interpretation* without saying why. Let me spend more time with it directly. What lies in the heart of interpretation? What animates it? What is the "anima" of interpretation? I will take the way of the word, for it gets to to the heart of the matter by leading me to it rather than my conforming it to my image. One of the reasons why I take pleasure in working with words in this way is that I learn something of the word's view of what I am up to. This softens that too-hard edge of always using words to explain something. Of all the discussions I have seen about interpretation, what it is, how to do it, and so on, I do not think I have seen one that begins with the sense of the hidden images embedded in the word itself.

The *inter-* element of the word refers to "among" or "between" with an emphasis on mutuality, that is, something done together. When we are true to the word itself, our interpretations will be something that is done together, rather than something done to someone or something. The *inter-* element implies a relatedness that is not hierarchical. It comes from a root which yields such other words as *inner, interior, intimate,* and that marvelous little word that the science of language calls the "copulative conjunction": *and.* In this sense, "and" is an eros word.

This implies that an interpretation would be an "and" to the dream, not a replacement, not an "or." The interpretation itself relating to the dream, a kind of "withness" with the dream, interpretation as a copulative conjunction, where the dream and interpretation together yield up a third thing. This I think is what Lopez-Pedraza is after when he urges us to "stick to the image."[74] Now that's a copulative image! A kind of "withness" that is not hierarchical, emphasizing a kind of conversation, not only between analyst and patient, but between dream and ego. "This *and* that," as Jung used to say. It is the absence of this andness, I believe, that Hillman objects to when the dream is taken too quickly into the day world, taken too soon into talking about how to solve an ego problem, where the interpretation takes up center stage and the dream gets forgotten once it has pushed us into our favorite topics.[75]

Now all of this is quite compatible with how we usually regard our interpretative moves. At least it seems a desirable image for interpretation. But *inter-* is not the main element of interpretation nor does it distinguish interpretation from other inter- words serving as the vocabulary of facts and fantasies of our work: interact, interchange, interest, interfere, interject, interlude, intermix, internalize, intern, interrelate, interrupt, intersect, interval, intervention, intercourse, and so on.

The crucial element in interpretation, that which distinguishes it from our other "inter" activities is the element *pre-*. It seems a common enough verbal element but actually is quite uncommon. It is not the *pre-* that means "before." Rather it is a quite rare root and one that has not been very productive or fertile in any language. Its literal meaning is "to traffic in," "to sell." In the

Greek this verbal root became the word περνημι, meaning "I sell" and developed into the Greek word πορνη, that is, "prostitute," and is the origin of our English word "pornography."

The word itself yields up this rather gross description of our work: selling intimacy, prostituting the interior, interpretation as a pornography of the inner world. This is very disagreeable! But it does provide a graphic hint as to why interpretation often yields nothing except the momentary relief of frustration, and why, so often, nothing is born of interpretation except dependency upon it.

Or, put another way, why analysts so often must prostitute their inner psychic reality in servicing the patient with techniques and methods of interpretation. After all, in prostitution one gets paid for satisfying the client, not oneself. Of course, the most disagreeable aspect of this "prostitute" image in the heart of interpretation is its literal enactment: when analyst becomes an actual prostitute and the patient pays for intercourse with the analyst. This may be claimed to be the work of eros, but I think not. It is more likely the literalization of interpretation *without* eros and invariably becomes the ultimate prostitution of psyche's desire.

When I discovered this root of πορνη in the word interpretation, I wondered about pornography itself and particularly about its "emergence" from hidden places in the past few years. What does pornography tell us? I'm not concerned with whether it should be available or not, or how it's used. I'm more interested in the images themselves and what they seem to be saying. Here again is one of those things that we may easily sit back and interpret. But what happens to psyche, what does psyche say when we put ourselves under pornography's influence? What does psyche say when in one of those shops or movies on 42nd Street or in the modern VCR bedroom?

Well, again, taking Barthes's interesting idea of the *punctum,* what is it that punctures one in these settings, what functions as *punctum?* One of the things that is *punctum* for me in watching such movies is that the ejaculation of the male must be *seen.* This is quite literally the climax of most every scene. It is this seeing of masculine ejaculations on the surfaces of women that is so striking. Pornography is respectable now as one of the sexual freedoms of recent decades and flourishes even more with the availability of home videotape systems. These images must have large appeal. I wondered: why are men seen spending their passion only on the surfaces of women? I was struck by the simple observation that however exciting this may be, however sexually stimulating seeing that seed on the surface, nothing creative can come from this. Fertilizing the surface is not a generative impulse. I thought, there can be no generation from this. I was startled to hear a response from my own interior that corrected me with a shout: "NO GENERATIONS!" The *plural* quality of this expression was striking. The visual dominant in our culture—is it "seeing is believing"?—forces the seeing of masculine seed on the surface of women. This we call "adult" or "X," but here the "X" is only for explicit and "all visible" not "X" as an unknown in an erotic algebra of the imagination. NO GENERATIONS!, my psyche echoed, saying quite literally, no generations can come from this. While pornography is called "erotica" and can be quite sexually exciting I don't feel there is much eros in it. It feels like a glorification or worship of the non-generative phallus. That is not eros. Aware of the close relationship between the word for masculine seed and the words themselves, it seemed to me that the same observation held true in our everyday speech or even more in the kind of "officialese" and "psychobabble" that characterize our conversations: words spilled excitedly on the surface of things: no generation! No generations!

My mind wandered into the relationship between this image in pornography (no generations) and prophylactics generally (no generations) and the relation of all this to the nuclear myth which has as its underlying image *no generations*. And I wondered whether our emphasis on freedom and choice (in life style, in sex, in abortion, in relationship) is motivated by a "freedom from the future," because the future as it approaches is sensed as so deeply intolerable. It is as if we are led to prevent or kill the life of the future in pursuit of an unburdened and pleasurable present, a present which is ever more clouded by a sense of futurelessness. In all those areas where we have now "won" freedom of choice, Eros seems to be missing. Again, the deepest question: Where is Eros?

It is true in our sex lives as well as in our word lives that something is failing to go deep enough. Pursuit of pleasure seems necessarily coupled with protection against generations. But is there genuine pleasure in this? I mean pleasure that goes deeply. I mean the kind of pleasure that comes as the child called Pleasure came, from a union of Psyche and Eros?

The phrase "I have no time" in its various forms has become so common, such a carrier in all aspects of our life, it is perhaps time that we began to listen to what we are literally saying: *we have no time.* We live under the triple burden of speed, surface, and survival. We are so busy surviving the pressures of modern life that we haven't the time to go beneath the surface, and we speed from one thing or person to another. Recall again what Wordsworth said when he saw this coming: "The world is too much with us."

Well, I want to believe that the approaching guest that Jung speaks of and that Freud called out to is Eros. It is said that Eros was born out of chaos (as well as poverty—*Penia*—his mother), and it is my sense that it is Eros, this dark urge, this father-mother of all creation, that approaches as the coming guest if for no other reason than that the *absence* and *poverty* of Eros is so stunning in our time. Freud referred to it when he said: "It is now to be expected that the great god Eros will come to do battle with the god of death." The god of death hovers over our world today, working its will toward the almost certain extermination of the world and its future through nuclear holocaust. What will do battle with this threat is not reason, not the rational intellect that Freud thought would calm the soul. No. What comes is not reason, rationality, intellect—much of that is caught up in, and in service to, Thanatos.

Here's a poet's vision of it:

> In a hand like a bowl
> Danced my own soul,
> Small as an elf,
> All by itself.
>
> When she thought I thought
> she dropped as if shot.
> 'I've only one wing,' she said,
> 'The other's gone dead,'

'I'm maimed; I can't fly;
I'm like to die,'
Cried the soul
From my hand like a bowl.

When I raged, when I wailed,
And my reason failed,
That delicate thing
Grew back a new wing,

And danced, at high noon,
On a hot, dusty stone,
In the still point of light
Of my last midnight.[76]

So, it is madness that will nurse psyche now, but not the madness caused by reason's distortions, not just craziness; nor will it be the madness encased in the cages of women's rage, nor the lunacy brought by the ancient goddesses returning. We must listen to psyche speaking in all these forms of madness. But what will nurse psyche now is the madness of eros, a myth in formation, the flame of that which saves love from time's destruction, it will be the madness known as...well, let's save its name for a time. Let's see if we can't find its verb before we are caught up too quickly by reason's need to name.

We have seen Jung's urging a listening to the spontaneous psyche, how art becomes a welcoming eros to the approaching guest. The centrality of the image of art in Jung's late thought contrasts sharply with Jung's views on modern art and modern literature, views which were quite condemning and rejecting. In 1937, he would say, "the artist of today assiduously avoids anything meaningful."[77] In 1947, he would write to Esther Harding, thanking her for a book she had sent, saying, "I don't know T. S. Eliot...If you think his book is worthwhile, then I don't mind even poetry. I am only prejudiced against all forms of modern art. It is mostly morbid and evil on top of that."[78] The book was *The Wasteland.*

But under the influence of Sir Herbert Read's defense of modern art, Jung began to change his feeling. By 1959, he would say: "What modern art represents is questionable. It is certainly something which transcends any hitherto valid form of understanding."[79] And you have heard his statements in the late correspondence.

If something in the nature of art holds for us the speech that is necessary in providing the welcoming eros for the coming guest, I do not believe it is only what we call artists that are to function as "mouthpieces," to use Jung's term, but something of the artist soul in each and every one of us. I do not believe we serve the developing eros very well if we only seek to interpret and understand the work of modern artists of whatever form. The developing eros is something that we each must participate in by listening, telling, and doing.

We are hampered, I believe, in a peculiar way by Jung's own relation to art. And because of this, and because the very late Jung attributes so much importance to art, I want to go into this question more deeply. I believe there is something crucial for us in the relationship between *art* and *eros* and *act*, something we need to hear.

Jung's Refusal

IN HIS *Memories,* Jung says of his early experiences in the period between 1912 and 1917: "All my works, all my creative activity, has come from those initial fantasies and dreams which began in 1912....Everything I accomplished in later life was already contained in them, although at first only in the form of emotions and images."[80] How did Jung cope with this deluge? He says: "My science was the only way I had of extricating myself from that chaos. Otherwise the material would have trapped me in its thicket, strangled me like the jungle creepers."[81]

Jung says it was his *science* that enabled him to deal with the chaos that was threatening him. Keeping this in mind, consider his description of one of these experiences, a time when the whole atmosphere of the Jung household was full of ghostly presences and bedeviled by a series of parapsychological phenomena. In the midst of that chaos, Jung broke out with the cry, "For God's sake what in the world is this."[82] And he was answered immediately in a chorus of voices: "We have come back from Jerusalem where we found not what we sought."[83]

With this Jung began to write out his conversations with these voices: "Then it began to flow out of me, and in the course of three evenings the thing was written....The haunting was over."[84] These conversations became *Septem Sermones ad Mortuos,* the "Seven Sermons to the Dead."[85] This is not science. It is not understanding. It is not scientific classification and description of images. It is conversations with the imaginal dead, which, as Jung says, "formed a kind of prelude to what I had to communicate to the world about the unconscious."[86] To me, when Jung took up the pen under the pressure of that chorus he was, like AE, more artist than scientist and it was the full-blown *expression* of what was visiting him—the *act* of writing it out—that dissolved the ghostly assemblage. It was *not* his scientific understanding of what he was experiencing. That was to come later and over the course of the next fifty years. That would be his science.

Earlier in the *Memories,* Jung describes another experience. At one point as he was writing down his fantasies he asked: "What am I really doing? Certainly this has nothing to do with science. But then what is it?"[87] It was crystal clear to Jung that writing down and picturing these experiences of autonomous voices and visions of "the spontaneous psyche" was not science. If anything, he thought they might be prelude to madness, or outright madness as some label such experiences. To Jung's amazement, his question was answered strongly by another spontaneous voice: "It is art."[88] Jung writes: "It had never entered my head that what I was writing had any connection with art."[89] He says, "I knew for a certainty that the voice had come from a woman."[90]

Earlier, when Jung described some of his first dreams and visions as he let himself plummet to the bottom of the psyche, he reported a dream in which Elijah had appeared with a blind girl named Salome.[91] And, writing of her in *Memories,* Jung says he was deeply *suspicious* of her. He says: "Salome is an anima figure. She is blind because she does not see the meaning of things. Elijah is the figure of the wise old prophet and represents the factor of intelligence and knowledge; Salome, the erotic element. One might say that the two figures are personifications of Logos and Eros. But such a definition would be excessively intellectual. It is more meaningful to let the figures be what they were for me at the time—namely events and experiences."[92] And at the time, Jung was deeply suspicious of this Salome, this blind companion to Elijah. For Jung to say that Salome is blind because she does not see the meaning of things has made me uneasy since the first time

I read it. Jung certainly needed no reminding that blindness need not interfere with seeing the meaning of things, but on the contrary was often a condition of such seeing, particularly seeing into the mysteries, "seeing with the eyes closed," as the word itself reminds us. I wrote in the margin of the book: "Jung seems blind himself to the meaning of this blind Salome." Jung certainly would have thought of John the Baptist beheaded at the behest of Salome for his refusal of her love; he would have known of her seven veils; he would have known of her popularity as a figure in art, music, and literature. And he would have thought too, I imagine, of that other Salome, Lou Andreas-Salomé, who had been so erotically entangled with Rilke and with Nietsczhe. She sided with Freud and opposed Jung at the Weimer Conference in 1911, just *before* Jung's confrontation with the unconscious.[93]

Jung says he was suspicious of the blind Salome in this early dream. He connects her with Eros and the erotic element and talks about how wise old men often have young ladies at their sides who they have taken from brothels. I presume Jung knew the meaning of her name. Does it come as a surprise to know that the Semitic root means "to be whole" and that in its Arabic form of *slama* it means "to be safe" and in its form as *salem* means "peace" and is found in such words as *Salaam, Islam, Moslem,* and of course, *Jerusalem.* His ghost chorus had said: "We have come back from Jerusalem where we found not what we sought." It appears in Hebrew as *Shalom* and *Solomon* and in its Greek form becomes *Salome,* meaning "peace." But clearly this blind Salome did not bring Jung any peace. It deeply disturbed him. It seems possible this young blind girl had a deeper significance than what seems to me a prejudice that she can't see the meaning of things.

At this point in Jung's reflections on these early experiences with the unconscious, he begins to describe his adventure with *Philemon* and *Ka*. For Jung, *Philemon* was the spiritual aspect, "meaning," while *Ka* seemed almost demonic, a kind of Mephistophelian earth or metal demon. Jung came to understand these two figures through his later work on alchemy. For Jung, then, *Philemon* can see meaning while blind *Salome* cannot.

It is after this discussion of *Philemon* and *Ka* that Jung tells the story of the woman's voice who answered his question "What am I doing?" with "It is art." Jung says that he recognized this voice as the voice of a patient, a woman patient, a talented psychopath, "who had a strong transference" to him. Of this figure, Jung said, "She became a living figure within my mind."[93] There has probably never been a clearer expression of the subjective experience of what we now call "countertransference" than this: "She became a living figure within my mind." If Jung was suspicious of a blind Salome, what must his feeling have been toward a woman patient, psychopathic and talented and with a strong erotic transference, who appears spontaneously in his mind, a living figure making pronouncements?[94] *Philemon, Elijah,* and *Ka* all had become living figures too; all had made announcements and pronouncements, all had brought strange and pagan ideas which Jung hardly understood at the time—much of which he put into paintings, drawings, elaborately scripted texts, experiences which could be rendered *only* in such forms. But to this voice, to this woman's voice, to just this voice, to what may be described as the first utterance of the anima in Jung's psychology, so obviously alive in his mind, what does Jung say? "Obviously what I was doing wasn't science. What then could it be but art? It is as though these were the only alternatives in the world. That is the way a woman's mind works."[95]

"That is the way a woman's mind works." Keep in mind this is Jung speaking almost fifty years later—but prior to his interchange with Herbert Read. Can he possibly mean what he says? Surely he could have said that is the way the anima's mind works or an animus even. But a *woman's* mind? I hope I'm not the only one who senses a problem here and I'm not referring only to the content of Jung's statement—"that is the way a woman's mind works." How I would love it— I think sometimes—if a woman's mind worked in only such an either/or way! One could after all figure that out after a time. No, what I want to point to is much simpler than that hornet's nest. I want to point out that Jung asked a question of the psyche and got a straight answer. "What am I really doing?" "It is art." It seems to me that it is Jung's ego that thinks "if it is not science it must be art." It is Jung's mind, not that of woman, who *on just this point* thinks this way. Jung continues and tells us what he answered back to the woman's voice:

> I said very emphatically to this voice that my fantasies had nothing to do with art, and I felt a great inner resistance. No voice came through, however, and I kept on writing. Then came the next "assault," and again the same assertion: "that is art." This time I caught her and said: "No, it is not art! On the contrary, it is nature." I prepared myself for an argument but there was none. When nothing of the sort occurred he writes I reflected that the "woman within me" did not have the speech centers I had. And so I suggested she use mine. She did so and came through with a long statement.[96]

Jung does not give us the voice's long statement, but he refers to it: "What the anima said seemed to me full of deep cunning. If I had taken those fantasies of the unconscious as art, they would have carried no more conviction than visual perceptions, as if I were watching a movie. I would have felt no moral obligation toward them."[97] What Jung reveals in this statement is his ego's perception of art and artists. It would be difficult to find an artist—any genuine artist—who could possibly accept such statements as applying to their experience. Any artist knows the driven quality the image moving toward birth brings. Jung knew this himself because he was literally forced to put those experiences into form. Any artist, too, knows that what is given birth through the artist makes tremendous demands and cannot possibly be equated with simply a passing movie. But this was Jung's conscious view, and it was out of this view that he responded to the anima's statement.

If these images are not art, or at least coextensive with the origins of art, what is it about the images that pushes Jung to stress the need to relate to the ethical obligation the images bring? Surely it cannot be his scientific attitude. I find Jung's thinking about all of this rather confused, as if a complex were at work. And like a complex, one cannot quit talking about it. So Jung continues to spin the tale of what might have happened *if* he had agreed with her: "The anima might then have easily seduced me into believing that I was a misunderstood artist and that my so-called artistic nature gave me the right to neglect reality."[98]

Well, the anima cannot seduce without an open door to seduction. Jung says he is seducible on this point, which once again points not to his understanding of art but his prejudices against it. He has a ready image for how the seduction would go: into being a *misunderstood* artist (why misunderstood?) and *neglectful* of reality (why neglectful?). How strange it is to find Jung now so readily understand by artists and so often misunderstood by scientists and how he stands accused of mystical pretensions that took him and take his followers away from any realistic relationship to reality.

Jung doesn't stop but, as if to nail down the last nail on the coffin of this voice, he says: "If I had followed her voice, she would in all probability have said to me one day, 'Do you imagine the nonsense you're engaged in is really art? Not a bit!' Thus, the insinuations of the anima, the mouthpiece of the unconscious, can utterly destroy a man."[99] Jung posits a future time, a time of having followed the anima's cunning seduction and tells us what she would have said. In other words, even if Jung had followed the voice, he feels it would have eventually turned on him like a virago, swallowing up his art and utterly destroying him. How *unlike* the letter to Herbert Read where Jung talks of the artist, not as "insinuating" mouthpiece, but as "mouthpiece" proclaiming the arrival of the coming guest!

But in that early time, the anima's simple expression that what Jung was doing was art was a threat and fell into Jung's own complexes of "being misunderstood," "neglecting reality," and "utter destruction" under the influence of the talented, if psychopathic, woman.

I believe Jung's attitude toward art and art's contribution to the eros problem has wounded our psychology, has left us uncertain and highly imitative, and lies at the root of some of our particularly Jungian difficulties with the anima and the feminine. I do not wish to diminish Jung in any sense. I cannot do that, for he has meant too much to me. It is because he has taught me to love the psyche that I must love it enough to see that the psyche's spontaneous expression, "It is art," perhaps the first self-conscious expression of anima *as* anima in our time, hides an enormous meaning that we must attend to and not reject.[100]

We are under no compulsion to be bound by Jung's entanglement—we are free to find our own. Hidden here in Jung's rejection not only of the blind Salome (that name that means wholeness and completeness—those values Jung so strived for), but of the talented, artistic, psychopathic woman, that erotic being who became a living figure in Jung's mind, hidden in these figures as they echo down through the history of our field, is the beginning of the way into a redemption of the artist soul, a work that lies at the root of our continual conflict over the science and art of analysis, a work that lies at the bottom of our continuing difficulties with the problem of the "clinical" versus "symbolic" basis of analysis. It is a work I believe Jung pointed to in that late letter to Herbert Read, where art is pictured as the mouthpiece proclaiming the coming age, the age of the coming guest. It is a work that needs to be undertaken by each of us or we shall soon find ourselves splitting apart, fragmenting from one another, and unable because of this to undertake the necessary task that lies before us.

Steel on Stone, Again

TO ME, Jung speaks as a poet when he says, "Life at the core is steel on stone." And at his tower, that "maternal womb" where he could "become what he was," it was Jung as sculptor who carved out those "rough answers" as he called them, carving into the stone walls with steel those concrete images of the psyche. I have become particularly interested in one of these carvings and want to tell you my musings on it. It was in the early fifties that Jung looked at a spot on the tower wall and saw in the contours of the stone a woman on her knees. Behind her was an image of an old king. As Jung began to carve the woman's figure, the image of the king vanished. Suddenly Jung saw in front of the woman the image of the hind quarters of a horse, a mare with distended teats as if full of milk. It was for this milk the woman was reaching. Into the body of the horse, Jung carved a Latin expression which in English becomes "May the light arise, which I have borne in my body."[101] Behind the figure of the horse, in Greek, Jung carved the expression: "Pegasus leaping forth—a consecrating gush of the water-carrier." On the other side of the kneeling female figure Jung saw a bear and carved it pushing a ball along with the Latin inscription: "The she-bear moves the mass."[102]

When Jung was asked to give an account of these figures in 1960, he said: "The whole thing, it seems to me, expresses coming events that are still hidden in the archetypal realm."[103] Obviously, these were not ideas Jung was consciously trying to put into stone. Rather, when he gazed at the stone, the stone "spoke" to him.[104] Jung "released" the images imprisoned there, brought them into view, into visibility. These are experiences any sensitive sculptor would recognize. In this sense, the artist is the means of liberation of images struggling for visibility not only in psyche but in all of matter as well! The images are alive, but imprisoned in matter. This, of course, is the Gnostic view which was so attractive to Jung. The eros act of the artist, of course, is the act of rendering visible. Jung was artist in the act of liberating these images from their anonymity in the stone. Of course, we can call all of this projection and argue about whether it is art, and it can be seen this way to be sure. But projection can never tell us why the image is not sufficient, why the image needs to be made into a reality in stone. Projection has no answer for that. The answer lies in eros and projection plays no part in eros.

Jung becomes scientist, speaks as psychologist when he talks *about* the images. Of the kneeling woman: "Obviously my anima in the guise of a millennia-old ancestress." Of the milk the woman reaches for: "milk, as *lac virginis*, virgin's milk, is a synonym for the *aqua doctrinaire*, one of the aspects of Mercurius." Of the mare: "Pegasus. I have represented it in its feminine aspect, the milk taking the place of the spout of water in the sign for Aquarius....Pegasus is the constellation above the second fish in Pisces....This feminine aspect indicates the unconscious nature of the milk." Of the purpose of this milk: "The milk has first to come into the hands of the anima, thus charging her with special energy." Of the bear: "The bear stands for the savage energy and power of Artemis." Of the ball: "Obviously this ball is being brought to the worshipper as a symbol of individuation. It points to the meaning and content of the milk."[105]

Something troubled me in Jung's description. At first I thought it was the disparity betweeen what he said were the *coming events still hidden* in the archetypal realm—an idea I could readily accept—and his seeming certainty about what the images were. There is little hiddenness in Jung's commentary. Where is that sense of Jung telling us the symbol is the only possible expression of something not yet fully known? I began to feel that Jung was almost parodying himself here—attaching names to the images as if the explanation might lessen one's looking too closely at the images themselves. Jung's careful description of each element is perhaps the clearest example of "Jungian" reductionism. Then I noticed that Jung did not say anything about the purpose of this scene. Yes, milk is a symbol for Mercurius; yes, such milk would charge the anima with special energy, mercurial energy, transformational energy; yes, the ball points to individuation and to the secret of the milk, but to what end? To what "coming events" still hidden in the archetypal realm does the milk point? Doesn't it seem Jung is talking about coming events *in the world?* Isn't this image in stone an augur's image?

Jung does say that the she-bear is linked with Russia and sets the ball rolling and that the anima has her mind on spiritual contents. Clearly one line of development in pursuing the implications of this image would be to go into the social-political world events of which Russia is instigator. Clearly that will have something to do with what we might call the individuation of the world. And are there signs that the anima is now charged with a special energy? We might more easily attach the charge not to anima but to women, for clearly since these images were carved women have been quite charged with special transformational power. Or, is it anima after all, in the sense that Marilyn Nagy brings up, that the current facination with the equation "feminine equals unconscious equals irrational equals myth equals poetry equals imagination equals life of psyche, sounds suspiciously more like an anima state of mind than it does like the material of feminine psychology?"[106]

Nagy brings up an important point. In response to Nor Hall's book, *The Moon and the Virigin,*[107] Nagy asks whether "the substance of my hope is to be the fact that I can experience the imaginative psyche—whether that's it—or whether there is real hope in that experience for a transformation of the realities of the ego. That was the main aim of Jung's psychology." As I have tried to make clear before, I cannot agree with this last statement. One purpose of Jung's psychology was surely the transformation of ego realities. But that was not the *main* purpose. The main purpose was *the incarnation of the realities of the Self.* The ego will not be transformed merely by experience of the imaginative psyche because the task is to bring the imaginative psyche into reality. If that equation is left suspended, if a route back into literal and material reality is not found, then nothing fundamental is ever accomplished.

Jung does not tell us what he felt about the disappearance of the old king. As the female figure began to materialize in the stone, the old king disappeared. It takes little imagination to assume Jung would speak of the death of the old king and its alchemical significance, namely the dying of the principle of the old order, the worn out principle of the passing Picean age, symbolized by a clearly patriarchal figure that disappears with the manifestation of the feminine body. The image of the king lost substance, it carried insufficient life to come out of the stone. It disappeared. This disappearance of the king in Jung's imaginal relation to the stone was announcing the demise of the patriarchy with the rising of the feminine. The common plaint ones hears these days: "Where are the men?"—a question the anima asks too!—may be linked with the disappearance of the king's image, for the king was the only male image to appear. Even that most masculine of creatures—Pegasus—Jung pictures in the feminine form. But do not forget. There is a masculine impulse in all this— *steel on stone*—Jung, the man, acting on the hint, making the image; that is the eros act.

When the old king disappears a mare appears. It is a mare whose teats the woman almost grasps. As Jung says, the image forced itself on him. He calls it "Pegasus." We know that Pegasus was many things but never a mare, never a female. As I was working on this image I was reminded again of my little limerick where I observed that "Maidie was not a ladie." And neither is Pegasus. This odd fact of the horse being female requires Jung, in interpreting it, to say:" I have represented it in its feminine aspect, with, moreover, the milk taking the place of the water in the image if the spout of water in Pisces." Clearly Jung attaches the whole scene to the transition from Pisces to Aquarius, and this idea forces an interpretation which speaks of Pegasus as a mare and milk as water.

I wondered what would happen if one stuck closer to the image itself, if one stayed a bit longer with the image of the mother horse, the nurse, the milk-full image of the mare. It would appear that the mother mare has given birth. Jung inscribes into the side of the mare: "May the light arise, which I have borne in my body." The statement refers to a "light" that has been born and the horse is offering a prayer that this "light" shine forth, "arise." With the female figure kneeling and reaching for the milk, it does not stray too far from the image to see the woman herself as what has been born, the woman herself as the light so long carried in the mare, and the woman herself to be nursed, and to shine forth, woman herself who shall rise up.

Surely, we could see this rising up of the feminine light as having its correspondence in the development of the women's movements of liberations in all their various forms. I would not want to dispute this. But I believe the image carries a deeper significance. I believe we get a deeper sense of what the image is pointing to and anticipating if we see the feminine figure as psyche. Psyche herself being nursed with the milk of some kind of animal. Jung's inscription relating to Pegasus, "Pegasus leaping forth—a consecrating gush of the water carrier," is very curious. Adler says it is a pun on the name of Pegasus which literally means "fount-horse" from the verbal elements "fount" and "gush forth."[108] But I don't believe Jung would inscribe a pun in such a deep-going image. Deep or dark humor perhaps, but not a pun. Rather, I think the significance of the fount-horse is overlooked and unstated. Remember first that Pegasus was born of the blood of the slain Medusa. What comes out of the death of that power that turns things into stone is Pegasus. When we speak of tradition and patriarchal power turning everything it touches into lifeless form, into stone in that sense, we are speaking of a kind of "Medusa look" that stands behind the patriarchy. The death of lifeless forms gives birth to Pegasus. That this idea is not just a fantasy is linked to Jung's use of the Greek word χον, which Adler has translated a "consecrating gush." Jung was certain to have known that this word was *only* used in reference to libations at funerals, a drinking, a kind of toast, to what has *died*. It is not at all to be confused with consecrating libations for the living or offerings to living gods. That is very definite. I'm sure Jung knew this. So, this gushing forth from "Pegasus" is partly an offering to what has died: a toast to the passing of the old king, the passing age of Pisces, and all of the dominants and traditions of that age.

More important yet is to remember that Pegasus was the one who with a blow of his hoof caused the fountain of the Muses to gush forth from the stones of Mount Helicon. And the name of this fountain is *Hippocrene* which means literally the "fountain of the horse." To drink of Hippocrene was the source of poetic inspiration. That is why Pegasus has always been a symbol of poetry. Even more directly we know that the great *goddess* of poetry and inspiration was pictured as a mare goddess, and her nurturant milk was the source of inspiration. Her name was *Aganippe,* a name which is related to words for "madness" and "night-mare." We are here close to the significance of that dream-poem: "Madness is psyche's only nurse," and why, possibly, a "dream wants a dream; a poem wants a poem." What the psyche is seeking in the transition from the Picean to the Aquarian age is the waters of Hippocrene, the milk Aganippe, of poetic madness, the source and nurse of inspiration. It is the voice of this inspired psyche, the psyche nursed by the milk of the Muses, that catches the ear of the artist soul and through the many acts of bringing forth creates that welcoming song to the coming guest. It caught Jung's eye, and he pictured it in stone. I like to think of this as his apology to the anima when he refused her first speech.

The image speaks to the intuition that Pegasus as the engendering source of the fountain of Muses is the link between the Picean "voice of tradition" and the Aquarian "voice of psyche." Pegasus breaks through the rocks of tradition bringing forth the creative and inspiring spring of the muses. In this sense the new age is not so much an age of consciousness as it will be an age of the poet—not the poet as noun, not the poet as career, but the *necessity* of poetry, the seeking by each one of us, a finding and drinking the waters and the milk of the Muses: poetry as verb, poetry as what we do. In this light, I find striking Harold Rosenberg's image of a time when:

> art consists of one-person creeds, one-psyche cultures. Its direction is toward a society in which the experiences of each will be the ground of a unique, inimitable form—in short, a society in which everyone will be an artist. Art in our time can have no other social aim—an aim dreamed of by modern poets, from Lautréamont to Whitman, Joyce, and the Surrealists, and which is embodied the essence of the continuing revolt against domination by tradition.[109]

Is the "Age of Aquarius" this "coming time"? Aquarius is pictured as a water bearer pouring water into a pool. I like to think of this as the image of the coming time when each and everyone of us brings to a common pool the water we have gathered from our unique and individual sources, from our encounters with the unconscious. By pooling together what we bring from these moments, by telling one another what we have experienced there, by acting on the hints we experience there, by doing these things, we will, I trust, begin to create that song of welcome to the coming guest.

These images are not on Jung's wall only. This process is alive in the psyche now. Perhaps you have seen it. One patient had this dream:

> I'm in the forest...in a clearing, and there is a circle of animals. It's as if I am one of them. It is very quiet, as if waiting for something. From somewhere I cannot locate there is a sound I can't make out. It's not exactly a voice or music. A voice behind me says: "Listen to this."

At that point the dreamer awoke. Since that time, her conscious efforts to reconnect with the sound have been carried on in the imagination and the sound is now clearly a poetic voice, a voice speaking out the numinous images of a time to come that now flow into her. The coming guest has found a "mouthpiece." Clearly, the animals are in the center place. The image Jung carved on his tower wall, and the compelling images in contemporary dreams, point to those animals as engendering a new birth.

PART THREE

Inner and Outer as Threads of One Weaving

In the deepest sense we all dream not out of ourselves but
out of what lies between us and the other.

—*C. G. Jung*

Words as Animals

NOT LONG before he died, and after the critical exchange with Sir Herbert Read that I have made such a point of, Jung received an abstract "modern" painting from a young artist who had sent it out of gratitude for Jung's work. Jung wrote back: "...the religious view of the world, thrown out at the front door, creeps in again by the back, albeit in strangely altered form—so altered that nobody has yet noticed it. Thus does modern art celebrate the great carnival of God."[110] Thus does Jung declare the purpose of art in the modern world, that is, to connect once again with "the great animals in the background who seem to regulate the world."[111]

Jung was always sensitive to animals and how they appeared in the world, in the imagination, in dreams. In his visions seminar he made one of those spontaneous remarks that contains insights that would just come to him, animal-like, under such conditions. He said: "Now the question is, why have the animals disappeared from the Christian teaching? When animals are no longer included in the religious symbol or creed, it is the beginning of the dissociation between religion and nature. Then there is no mana in it. As long as the animals are there, there is life in the symbol; otherwise, the beginning of the end is indicated."[112]

I kept thinking of Jung's oft-repeated statement that the world hangs by a thread and that this thread is the psyche. I kept envisioning the fraying of these threads and was struck by what seems to be a gathering tide of apocalyptic dreams, dreams picturing catastrophic events of all manner and description, occurring widely even in individuals not given to such images. I have observed the common elements of an extraordinary event in preparation, a sense of imminence, and, most peculiarly, a remarkable sense of acceptance of it all as just so. The one thing that has kept me from being overly depressed and resigned, the one thing that seems to me hopeful in these apocalyptic visions from the unconscious, is a simultaneous and increasing appearance of animals, animals coming, animals watching, animals speaking, animals wanting to lead us, animals undergoing all manner of transformation. To reconnect to the animal, we must become aware of the animals in the psyche, the animal psyche, the animal in things, the animal in art, in words, in poems, in dreams, the animal that lies between us and the other.

Of course, the fate of Jungian psychology pales in significance when confronted with the deeper question of the fate of the world and the fate of the psyche. These powerful concerns created enormous expectations in me relating to these lectures—expectations impossible to fulfill. My hopes for psyche to speak to this task of contributing "original work" to the development of Jungian psychology seemed continually dashed. The woods and the river and the animals seemed to pull me more strongly, and what did that have to do with the fate of the world? It seemed my psyche was revolting at attempts to bring some new development, some original work, kept rebelling in the most varied ways, would not cooperate, as if the truly important work was not this, not this seeking after some advancement in Jungian thought. "No Jungian lectures," my dreams screamed! In facing these questions and issues, I seemed to pale and felt as if I were losing blood for the task. How thoughtful, I thought, that the sponsors would arrange for me to speak in the New York Blood Center! Perhaps I could arrange for an infusion.

But surely the inauguration of the C. G. Jung lectures would require a Jungian lecture. But how could I, who so often tells others: "Trust the psyche," how could I go against what psyche was shouting? So, I pondered: what is a *Jungian* lecture? When Jung spoke, of course, he could give a proper Jungian lecture because it was Jung speaking. His name referred to himself, carried his substance, had a definite place and sense. Since Jung's death, his name has become an adjective without a definite reference. Now we have Jungian analysts, Jungian patients, Jungian books, Jungian societies, Jungian communities, and Jungian lectures. If recent commentators are correct in their analyses that the idea of the unconscious proceeds from a noun stage, through an adjective stage, and finally to an adverb stage, then it will not be surprising one day to find "Jungianly" entering our vocabulary. He lectures so Jungianly! I find this very oppressive.

At the root of this is what I call the seduction of nouns and adjectives leading into a *separatist* language, a language in the service of rationality and linearity, insisting on subject-object distinctions. Its aim is distance, its style is prose, its claim is science, its anima is progress: getting somewhere. The language of such separation is made in sentences. But what do sentences sentence us to? Something is imprisoned in the sentence, and it yearns to be free. That freedom is found sometimes in poetry, where verse is free, where the sentence has lost its power, its throne. Poetry's language is verbs, vital and vivid verbs forcing involvement, inviting relationship rather than separation, immersion rather than distance. One can get a sense of the crucial difference this makes by exposing oneself to another language—particularly a language that is ideographic rather than phonetic—such as the Chinese.

Consider a small example. I have already mentioned the prominent place given "is" constructions in our psychological language. "That kneeling woman *is* my anima," Jung says. Feel the prominence of the *is*. Feel the sense of "translation." Feel the sense of "naming," pointing at. Where is the sense of relationship except in the act of naming? All our words come basically from the experience of acting, and for this reason the roots in all languages are primitive verbs. So every noun and every other part of speech is rooted in a verb. That is where the eros is. How would you draw a picture of "is"? In the Chinese language, "is" must be pictured and drawn. Like abstract art, we do not have eyes to see in Chinese. Yet, the picture is always an image of a relationship between concrete elements in action. The Chinese figure is very concrete: "is" pictured as a hand reaching for the moon almost touching it. The images are not hidden in Chinese; etymology always visible; every word clearly a poem. Yet, in English, our verbs are weak. We say "to shine." Or, if we want the adjective, we say "bright." Or if we want a noun we say "luminosity." Or if we try to be concrete we say "sun" but then we lose all sense of embodied act, no sense of animal. No eros there.

But one can get to the eros in words, the animal in words, by discovering the images hidden beneath the shell of words. When you reach this erotic layer in language you begin to experience the poetry in language, the poetry from which words spring, *poesis*, a fundamental poetry where psyche and world are one, the land Lorca's rose seeks. In our language one way to achieve this is by recovering the lost etymology, the underground roots, and, in a sense, playing with the language, and, in the deepest sense, *loving* the language in all the senses of love one can imagine. *That* way with language would help us to connect with "the great animals in the background who seem to regulate the world."

A Carnival of Images

WHAT IS MEANT by *enactment* in relation to a dream? Here's an example from my own experience. I dreamed of a cavern or hole of some kind on the land around my home. Out of a small opening in the cavern came a strange light—not bright, not flickering as a candle might, but a quivering luminous glow. That was the dream—just seeing this. That morning I walked around outside not quite knowing what to expect but keeping my eyes open for something. What finally caught my eye was a stone that had been broken so that the light of the sun was caught in its various surfaces and it shimmered with light. I sat down on the ground next to it, watching. I don't know how much time passed. After a while I could feel something change. I looked up and just a few feet away stood a fox. It was watching me. I watched the fox. After a time, watching done, the fox turned and walked away, looking back several times until disappearing into the trees. The kind of consciousness engendered by being face to face with a fox is rather different from talking about the fox as a symbol of something—even a symbol for the "slyness" for which the fox is famous and which is the meaning of Russell, my name. After the fox left I fell into looking at the rock again and then at the sun. Here is what I wrote later that day:

87

I have learned well that the sun is a symbol of consciousness. But what is it that pushes now to reverse this; what is it to want to write that "consciousness has become a symbol for the sun"? Remember that dream years ago looking out the window at the sun and reaching up and touching its image on the glass and being frightened that the sun on the glass was cold? Outside, today, in the sun, not talking *about it*, I didn't even have to reach. The sun's heat was on my fingertips if I just showed them to the sun. Its light comes to me. What images began to come then! What a carnival! Now I know why Bly said if one wants to write a pine-tree poem you'd better sit next to one. Then you can experience the consciousness in things themselves. That is not projection; it's perception! If matter and psyche are one, as Jung's work points to, can we really believe we are the only life with psyche? But what does the dream mean? I don't know. In some way the question took a back seat as I became busy with what psyche was spontaneously bringing. Memories like animals are returning. Like that story I started when I was fourteen, that story called "When Dreams Stopped," telling what happened to the world when there was no more time for dreams. The dreams rebelled by disappearing from memory, and the world was without dreams for generations. Then a young boy began to experience strange memories from out of his sleep, and his worried parents took him to specialists and they determined that he was mad. He would talk nonsense about animals speaking, about trees speaking, about plants speaking and by listening he seemed to know things before they happened in the world. But by then everyone had forgotten what a dream was. I didn't know how to finish the story then. I'm not sure I do now. But I will.

By "enacting the dream" I do not mean "play-acting" the parts of the dream, but connecting the dream through an act consciously undertaken in the world. The ego, of course, must be in position to be responsible for the act one undertakes. Another example. While on a trip to Scotland, I was fortunate to spend an evening with the great Gaelic poet, Somheirle MacGill-Eain (Sorley MacLean).[113] We had talked about poems of his and other Scot poets that had found their source in dreams. That night I had a dream in which I was at an old handpress and I was printing. The dream spoke of printing a book called *Moon Stone*, a book devoted to the "mystery of words." I have now acquired an old handpress and have set about printing books.[114] I can feel a yearning to make a place for hearing our collective dreams and their poetry, a place for the "reenchantment" of the world. To have psyche's speech heard only in consulting rooms will not suffice in the time to come. Psyche's voice must be heard in the world, enacted, incarnated in the world.

Seeing the brochure announcing these lectures, someone asked me what I meant by "psyche speaks." One of the things I mean is this. On my trip to the Western Highlands of Scotland I went in search of old storytellers. I wanted to hear stories first hand from still living storytellers, where storytelling was not a "career" but an organic part of the life of the community. A professor at the School of Scottish Studies in Edinburgh had given me some names and places. So off I went with my trusty tape recorder. I met first with an old man of nearly a hundred years in a rest home on the Island of Mull. He took me to his little room, rummaged about for the hidden bottle, and after two or three chugs together, we got down to business. I told him I wanted stories, and with his permission, turned on the tape-recorder, sat back, and listened. He was quite silent. We looked at each other for quite some time. Finally he asked me to pour another round and when I reached over to do so he whispered in my ear, "Turn that thing off." I did. "You know, in my day we didn't have those devils." Then he reached for a book on his night stand. It was a book of his stories all recorded, transcribed, and beautifully published by the School of Scottish Studies. "Oh, then, you've already told all your stories." "Not a one," he shouted, and he threw the book to the floor. "Those are ghosts, dead. My stories are here." He pointed to his ear and then his tongue and said, "and in my breath."

For more than four hours he told me stories until he fell into sleep. They were so alive in his memory. So alive in his breath. It was a carnival pouring out! He taught me there is something crucial in hearing and telling, something essential to psyche in our time, whether in story, dream, or poem, in the telling, in the hearing. I have no interest in explaining these stories. I won't even write them down. The School of Scottish Studies has seen to that. I could add an illuminating Jungian commentary, but I have no heart for it. This experience with an old man on Mull changed something in me, and the old man didn't even *know* that the Greek word for psyche comes from the root for breath, yet he realized this more deeply than I ever will. Those stories in his mind, in his memory, in his heart—we don't know that anymore. Everything is written down—even dreams. What do we remember now? Can we really remember psyche? What do we sing together now? Where is that feeling that poetry and song and story are not only in books? Where is that "blood-remembering" that Rilke[115] said would be essential to our survival? Is there poetry in our blood?

How to "write down," how to print books with the "mysteries of words," how to publish *Psyche Speaks* without losing the essential animal nature of psyche speaking in the breath, and that breath traveling to innocent ears; how indeed! That is a deep puzzle. Intuition tells me that the answer, at least for me, is finding the way to enact that little dream: "a dream wants a dream; a poem wants a poem."

I have been enormously intrigued by Kerenyi's dedication of his book, *The Heroes of the Greeks,* not to mythographers or scientists of the future, but "To the poets of the future."[116] But in the modern world we are far from the poets and the poets are far from the public. What was once the daily song and story of the people is now relegated mostly to little magazines, university squabbles, or entertainment, or resurrected through the back door in our therapies as we try to remember these things.

People used to have poems and songs and tales and stories in the memories—not forced to memorize as in school because their psyche was full of these things and the people lived it in their daily life. Community was bound together by the organic necessity of its poetry and by its art. When these things were written down it was the beginning of the end of a kind of psychic memory and psychic act and is now mainly something we do (read) in isolation from one another. As Jung says of Christianity, the animals seem to be lost in most of what is written now. And soon, when all of our memory can so easily be put into a computer chip, what will we be remembering then? What of the animal then?

We are approaching a truly revolutionary time when that great principle of human evolution will have achieved a new stage. I mean that principle that through thought and invention man does not have to physically evolve himself in adaptation to his world as do the animals. This frees him from evolution's sap; from his animal kin. Man does not need to physically evolve wings: he can fly without wings because he can invent machines to carry him. Not only can he adapt to his world in this way, he can adapt the world increasingly to his own vision. And when he turns this thought-based adaptation on himself, he begins to make machines to do everything he himself can do, as if in some curious way to replace himself. And to what end? Ideally, that should free mankind to concentrate on those areas where his adaptation has lagged behind his adaptation to the physical world: relating to himself and to his fellow human beings. That would be the embodiment of eros. The animating myth of science is progress and is the promise of ever newer golden ages where menial work will not exist, where all basic human necessities will be provided by machine. A time when disease and poverty will be only a memory. Perhaps then we will have time for psyche.

But there is a way to go yet before such a golden age, and, as Wordsworth said, "The world is too much with us." And when the world is too much with us, it's difficult to hear what poetry is saying, to see what art is picturing, to hear what dreams are after. This is particularly true when we listen with ears ready to explain what we hear rather than to listen to what the poem or the dream induces in us, to attend and care for the act the dream points to. A poem wants a poem; a dream wants a dream. How the poet would love to speak in such a way to rouse the poet in you; how the architect of dreams must yearn for something similar. In this sense we should wonder about ourselves if we await too eagerly the poet's next poem or our next dream. We should wonder what has become of our own as response.

I don't mean this as *therapy*. Therapy has usurped the once-primary place of poetry. We need therapy when we cannot sing, dance, or make art an integral part of our everyday life. In earlier time it was poetry that was the *terpnos logos,* the healing speech. The sick called not the physician—known then as those of "silent tongue"—but the poet, those of "willing tongue"! The fact that art, song, movement, dance, and poetry have all become "therapies" is a testament to the *reversal* that our culture of intellect and power has achieved. What was the source of the very binding together of culture has been so unravelled that it all must now be imported as therapy. So in therapy we are trying to sew back together huge tears in the fabric of the spontaneous life of psyche. And it is in principally these things that psyche now finds its nourishment. All these things have a tinge of madness about them and they are the first to be sacrificed at budget time. Everywhere! But we might be wary of putting our money into them until we have a better relation to money itself. In fact, we may need to find ways to accomplish these things without money. Dreams and poems come to us free. No charge. Gifts of nature really. We have something yet to learn from this. Our ultimate freedom lies in our binding ourselves to these things—that is the way of eros. Binding ourselves to the images of freedom that money promises is the great illusion of our time. No true freedom lies in that direction.

If we don't find ways to listen to the spontaneous psyche and sing it out to be heard, we will approach that state of "endless retailing of accumulated knowledge" that Hartman speaks of. A state in which we read Jungian reviews of things and miss the things themselves as when I discovered most everyone I knew had read Edinger's *Moby Dick,* but not Melville's. The purpose of art is to move us to new psychic ground; the endless effort to bring art under the wing of our science is detrimental first when it blunts our raw psychic involvement in art's vision and what that induces in us, and second when it attempts to reduce the work to old ideas. For art, unlike criticism or interpretation, is rooted in the future, its engine is the symbol which is the best possible expression of something not yet known. The purpose of art is to open us to the reception of the symbol as it moves through and in the objective psyche and, ideally, to recruit our response to the symbol. This is an embodiment of eros. Remember Beaudelaire: "The only proper criticism of a work of art is another work of art."

AE's Augury

I N 1884, the diphtheria bacillus was isolated, Mark Twain published *The Adventures of Huckleberry Finn,* and George Eastman developed his machine to make paper rolls of photographic film, thus enabling the camera to enter everyday life. At the same time, a young man of 17, walking the country roads of Ireland, began to experience vivid images flickering in his brain. As Jung would do a quarter of a century later, the young man set about painting the images he experienced and brooded on them. As he brooded, something "ancient and eternal seemed to breathe through" the images, and as we have seen earlier, the breathing became a distinct voice whispering: "Call it the Birth of Aeon." In reflecting on these experiences, his first encounters with the spontaneous psyche, AE wrote:

> I believed then, and still believe, that the immortal in us has memory of all its wisdom, or, as Keats puts it in one of his letters, there is an ancestral wisdom in man and we can if we wish drink that old wine of heaven. This memory of the spirit is the real basis of imagination, and when it speaks to us we feel truly inspired and a mightier creature than ourselves speaks through us. I remember how pure, holy and beautiful these imaginations seemed, how they came like crystal water sweeping aside the muddy current of my life, and the astonishment I felt, I who was almost inarticulate, to find sentences which seemed noble and full of melody sounding in my brain as if another and greater than I had spoken them....I am

convinced that all poetry is, as Emerson said, first written in the heavens, that is, it is conceived by a self deeper than appears in normal life, and when it speaks to us or tells us its ancient story we taste of eternity and drink the Soma juice, the elixir of immortality.[117]

AE had spent years practicing what we would now call active imagination, that is, achieving a state of mind in which images occur spontaneously without the preconception or agency of the ego and, most importantly, taking up an active relationship with the image. AE would focus on a dream image or even a geometrical pattern until psyche would "speak" in sound or image. It is through this early and continual practice, long before Jung was to enter this same country of active imaginal reality, that AE was exposed to experiences that have, like Jung's, considerable collective importance. As we have seen, Jung carved into his wall the expression "Let the light that I have carried in my womb shine forth." This points to a birth. AE's voice had whispered many years before: "Call it the Birth of Aeon." It is not too far a leap to consider these experiences anticipations of the coming age, the coming aeon, the aeon of Aquarius. Because Jungian psychology has paid no attention to AE, I would like to quote him again, to quote his major augury of the coming time:

I was meditating....in a little room, and my meditation was suddenly broken by a series of pictures which flashed before me with the swiftness of moving pictures in a theatre. They had no relation I could discover to the subject of my meditation....I was brought to a wooded valley beyond which was a mountain, and between heaven and earth over the valley was a vast figure aureoled with light, and it descended from that circle of light and assumed human shape, and stood before me and looked at me. The face of this figure was broad and noble in type, beardless and dark-haired. It was in its breadth akin to the face of the young Napoleon, and I would refer both to a common archetype. This being looked at me and vanished, and was instantly replaced by another vision, and this second vision was of a woman with a blue cloak around her shoulders, who came into a room and lifted a young child upon her lap, and from all Ireland rays of light converged on that child. Then this disappeared and was on the instant followed by another picture in the series; and here I was brought from Ireland to look on the coronation throne at Westminster, and there sat on it a figure of empire which grew weary and let fall the sceptre from its fingers, and itself then drooped and fell and disappeared from the famous seat. And after that in swift succession came another scene, and a gigantic figure, wild and distraught, beating a drum, stalked up and down, and wherever its feet fell there were sparks and the swirling of flame and black smoke upward as from burning cities. It was like the Red Swineherd of legend which beat men into an insane frenzy; and when that distraught figure vanished I saw the whole of Ireland lit up from mountain to sea, spreading its rays to the heavens as in the vision which Brigid the seeress saw and told to Patrick.[118]

I can only encourage anyone who might read these quotations here to take up AE's *The Candle of Vision* in its entirety as one way to connect with a major precursor of the "Jungian" view of the psyche and, perhaps, as one way of enlivening one's present experience of the psyche. Here is AE's commentary on his vision:

All I could make of that sequence was that some child of destiny, around whom the future of Ireland was to pivot, was born then or to be born, and that it was to be an avatar was symbolised by the descent of the first figure from the sky, and that before that high destiny was to be accomplished the power of empire was to be weakened, and there was to be one more tragic episode in Irish history. Whether this is truth or fantasy time alone can tell. No drums that have since beaten in this land seem to me to be mad enough to be foretold of in that wild drumming. What can I say of such a vision but that it impressed me to forgetfulness of analysis, for what it said was more important than any philosophy of its manner. I have tried to reason over it with myself, as I would with a sequence of another character, to deduce from a sequence better than could be done from a single vision, valid reasons for believing that there must be a conscious intellect somewhere behind the sequence. But I cannot reason over it. I only know that I look everywhere in the face of youth, in the aspect of every new notability, hoping before I die to recognise the broad-browed avatar of my vision.[119]

Slaying on Mad. Avenue

WHAT DO THE BIRDS SAY? I brought the mail in and went to sit on the deck to see what had come. All the usual stuff. And the first printed brochure announcing these lectures. And as I read it, a bird flew out of the trees, flew straight into the plate glass window in front of me and killed itself. Well, even an apprentice augur knows: *that* is a sign. In the language of augury this was an *oblativa,* an event "freely given" by the gods—no asking, praying, looking out for, or otherwise seeking. It was just presented. This contrasts with *impetrativa,* which are events specifically asked for (e.g., I hope I have a dream about this tonight.). I certainly wasn't asking for a bird to kill itself this way. So it was "freely given" by the gods: a bird killing itself as I read the announcement of these lectures. A synchronicity to be sure.

I didn't much like the feeling of being an augur. A few hours before I gave the after-dinner talk at the Annual dinner of the C. G. Jung Foundation of New York, a year and a half before this synchronicity, I was walking down 42nd Street and an old man collapsed right in front of me, right at my feet, just died. That night I was to talk about "Strange and Weird Experiences," telling some of my own experiences, particularly involving synchronicity, and stressing the general idea that the *fateful* quality one feels in synchronistic experience can be revealed even more fully by finding the links between synchronistic experiences. That is, it is hard to see—but not hard to feel—the significance of any particular synchronistic experience. But if you attend to a *series* of synchronistic experiences, you will begin to see a pattern to the inner and outer events woven together in time. Look for the pattern in synchronistic phenomena over time. There you will see the threads of your fate right before your eyes.

That man died at my feet, just before my talk. Then, one morning as I was on my way back from Grand Central Station, walking to the Foundation offices, where later that day I would tell the lecture committee about what I was going to talk about in these lectures, there, right in front of me, just a few yards away, I saw a young man shot and killed. Murdered right in front of my eyes. I wrote it out this way:

> I've always had passion for donuts
> and though a donut shop is not a church exactly
> I've experienced communion there
> even in that busiest little shop
> at Madison and Forty-second—my favorite—
> I walked past there yesterday
> yes, past it—had my donut already
> at Grand Central and you can't go
> to two churches after all
> even on Saturday.
>
> That meant months would pass
> before I took communion there again
> and a quiet sadness took hold of me
> broken into by a city sound
> louder than a trumpet
> and blood dripped through his hands
> poured I guess would be more exact
> as he staggered through his final seconds
> before his face felt the street
> too obviously dying or even dead.
> I'd never seen someone murdered before.
>
> Believe me TV does not prepare you
> for bloody hands
> that had given me
> donuts at other times,

not giving me communion now,
too busy clutching his last pain.
Was he wondering what it meant?
And I looked up into the eyes of his father
and his brother as they saw what I was seeing.
Etched on my eyes forever is that scene.

Imagine! The server of my passion murdered there
before my eyes—"Slaying on Mad. Avenue" screamed
the *Daily News* complete with picture and with my
foot in the corner of the photograph—my foot
forever now standing in that place, standing
there not knowing what to do, suddenly not wanting
to do anything, yet for an instant knowing I was alive
knowing too somehow my fate and his are intertwined
knowing now that I would tell of this in those
talks I do some months from now
knowing too I'll dedicate my talks about psyche
to that boy whose dreams have stopped.

Shortly after, Philip Zabriskie, then president of the New York Foundation, called me one evening to read back to me the final draft of the brochure material and during the course of that conversation told me that one of the old assistants at the Foundation had died there that day in the Foundation building.

Well, these were the first memories that flashed before me as I picked up the dead bird and went to put it in the ground. An old man dies. An elderly woman dies. A young man is murdered. A bird kills itself. All in connection somehow to my speaking in New York. "No Jungian lectures," my dreams insisted. This was enough to give me great pause. Many times I was close to cancelling. I wondered if I would live to do the lectures. I did. But on the day I received the first copies of the tapes of the lectures, almost impossible to listen to with all the static over my voice, on that day, my mother died. So it is not without some considerable unease that these lectures are here put into printed form.

Everything Belongs

I WAS ASKED ONCE by someone if I could capture the essence of Jung's psychology in a single phrase. I said yes and waited. This waiting is not being "lost in thought." What I experience is a kind of intuitive panic—I'm waiting for an intuition. Only *then* can I think. I never know how long it will take—hence a certain panic and sometimes an embarassment when nothing comes! Finally, it came: *everything belongs*. I think this "belongingness" quality of Jung's psychology is the source of its eros possibilities. So, from this perspective, all these deaths belonged.

"Psyche Speaks" suddenly had a haunting companion: "The world speaks too." I wrote out what came to me as I suffered the weight of these two refrains:

> Projection energizes the world. Reclaiming the energy of projection takes energy from the world. This is the major factor in becoming conscious and is the principal achievement of what Jung called "reflection." What remains as the vehicle for energy *into* the world when projections are withdrawn? Is there not a way for the world to call to psyche in ways other than projection? I believe so. I believe this would be the work of Eros, the world calling to us, bringing us and it together. Inner and outer as threads of one weaving. This is the difference I've felt between Eros and Hermes. Hermes is a god of projection. Taking psychic substance—the message—from one place to another. Projection as messenger. Taking, for example, the

iconography of the father from the patient's psyche and clothing the analyst with it—and all such. The return message, the counter message, is the countertransference, projection returning other projections, as one message responds to another. I don't think Eros is in this at all. Perhaps that's why erotic transferences seem not genuinely erotic in *feeling* but bring that driven eroticism so typical of the Hermes trickster. Eros does not work in projection. Eros works to move *both* individuals to a new realm. Transference as projection moves the participants only into what amounts to recycled enactments of lost objects, to constant mimesis of the past, a kind of cloning. Eros always works toward new ground in both, unknown, unfamiliar, and always having to do with the future. This is the probable meaning of the unknown quality in a symbol. Eros resides there.

Jung said, "Eros becomes not transference, not ordinary friendship or sympathy, but more primitive, more primeval, more spiritual than anything we can describe. It is immediate presence, as if we were mixed together in some way."[120] And it must apply to our relation to the dream and the poem—perhaps all art—as well. Perhaps that is what Jung is getting at when he says that "in the deepest sense we all dream not out of ourselves but out of what lies between us and the other."[121]

I was reminded of that scene in Edwin Muir's autobiography—the only autobiography I know other than AE's that rivals Jung's in depth and openness to psyche—that scene where in a walk about Glasgow he happened upon a crowd standing around two men. One man "who looked serious and respectable and not particularly angry raised his fist slowly every now and then, as if objectively, hit the other man, who stood in silence, and never tried to defend himself." A bystander asked him: "Why dinna you let the chap alane. He hasna hurt you." To which the serious young man replied: "I ken he hasna hurt me, but I'm gaun tae hurt him." Now this is not what I remembered so much as what the great Scots poet said of it: "The scene and particularly the words of the serious young man—the other said nothing at all—took hold of my mind as if they were an answer to some question which, without my knowing it, had been troubling me."[122]

That's what the bird's crashing into the glass, and all the other deaths, felt like to me—the answer to a question which, without my knowing it, had been troubling me. These are subtle weavings of inner and outer feelings of a reality that cannot be confirmed by anyone else because they are unique moments. To interpret such moments as "projection" I believe fundamentally abuses the eros nature of such interweavings with the world. A poet is, perhaps, fortunate because he has the fortitude to assert and access to a word well that can give voice to such realities. But this inter-penetration of psyche and world verges on the very definition of madness: the incapacity to distinguish and keep separate inner and outer reality. It will be ages, of course, before the discoveries of micro-physics—that point to psyche and matter as one—begin to penetrate consciousness in general.

It is, of course, keeping such things separate and silent, and "being silenced" for such experiences that turns them eventually into what we call madness. How we need to hear these things now! But we need willing ears for that. Have you ever wondered about the ear, wandered about the ear?

Madness in the Ear

THE EAR BEGINS with what is called the outer ear, the auricle, the pinna, the external acoustic meatus. How your imagination must be inspired, inflamed! But wait. Slow down. Hear these words more deeply. Auricle is "an open central court," especially in an ancient Roman house. Pinna is a feather, a wing, the word from which our word pen as writing instrument came, a word related to the Latin *petere*, from which we get "appetite." Ah! Appetite of the ears, giving the ears wings, writing with a feather, for the ear. How I would love these words to be admitted to the courtyard of your ear. Science has named this wing, this court yard, the external acoustic meatus? Meatus? What is this meatus? A blank word, all surface until you mine underneath this word, undermine it. Then you discover it is "a passage," from a root meaning "to change," a root from which the Old English *gemad* comes. What is this *gemad*? It means "insane" and is the source of our English word "mad." Ah! Madness in the ear! Madness was clearly associated with "change" (archaic echoes are preserved in the image of "changeling"), the passage from one state to another; normality with "staying the same." And once again this curious connection of madness and money. So there is a madness connected with the ear, right there at its outer courtyard, its wing, that passage into the interior.

And once in that passage, the word travels to the middle ear that space between *tympanum* and the *inner ear.* The tympanum is a drum and comes from a root meaning "to push, knock, beat." These words are in your ear beating, knocking, pushing on your drum. And are you surprised that from this root also arises the Greek word Styx, that River of Hades? Can't you sometimes hear the screaming souls in your ear? "Sticks and stones may break my bones but words will never hurt me!" Don't believe it! There is much wounding in the ear. A Hades there. But more, that space is filled with three little bones, the *malleus,* the *incus,* the *stapes.* You remember this from school. All just words, words for speed, for surface, for understanding. But malleus is a hammer and incus is an anvil and stapes is a stirrup, a brace for the foot. Why a brace for the foot? Is someone crippled there? How can you supress the image of the blacksmith, and if the blacksmith, can lame Hephaestus be far behind? Hephaestus, the smith, the craftsman, the magician, maker of Pandora, the first woman. Ah! Rilke's woman in the ear. Is a woman being crafted in these middle regions of your ear from these words I throw to you? What are you making from my words?

To the inner ear. First we enter the *vestibule,* that is, a small entrance hall, and you will remember Vesta in this name. Yes, Vesta is there, the hearth goddess. A hearth in the ear! Is it Vesta's temple right there in the ear? Is that the place where is kept the fire known as *ignis inextinctus,* the fire that must never go out or the town dies. The place of the Vestal Virgins, guardians of the deepest secret. The Vestal Virgins were also inaugurated by Numa, that same king who began the *Augures.* What does the ear have to do with augury. Yes. You've already said it: "A little bird told me!" And there, after the vestibule, we come to the *cochlea* hiding in its name a snail, that slow crawler not interested in speed: that spiral-shaped tissue which is a bed for the nerve endings essential for hearing. It is the brushing of the sound waves across the body of those endings that transforms sound waves into the chemistry of hearing. From the vestibule we arrive at the *semicircular canals,* those turning tubes so essential to the equilibrium of the body. The ears keep the body stable and are essential for our sense of balance and orientation. And if we are "unbalanced" and "disoriented" we call that madness. This is the area called the labyrinth of the ear.

Wandering through the ear this way sets me to wonder: what is this spiral necessity at the innermost geography of hearing? At the root of this image of spiral, from its word root, is an image of a woven basket. What did the Vestal Virgins keep in those woven baskets behind the curtain to which no one was allowed entrance and about which there is no knowledge at all? What secret lies still in this innermost chamber of the ear? Can you guess it?

Between Living and Dreaming

W E ARE APPROACHING the end, but there is a bit more to tell. Telling is not "talking about." Talking about goes forever in circles. Telling goes deeper. It is as I once called it: an *apocalypse of the interior*—not in the sense of destruction—but in the deeper meaning of the word: "to reveal oneself to another fully." Telling is related to bearing witness, more related to story than to explanation. Let's see how this difference is carried into the images of the words themselves. We know that explain means "to define, explicate, make comprehensible," as any dictionary will make clear to you. In fact, when we look up a word in the dictionary, we are seeking just that: we want the word defined, its meaning explicated, and its sense made comprehensible. We want the word to "make sense." And these definitions we look for are numbered and ordered: early to modern, popular to esoteric, central to peripheral. It is no wonder—and I mean simply there is no *wonder* in it at all— that definitions and meanings appeal to our sense of order, comprehension, understanding.

For me Jung's secret is that "everything belongs," and for this reason, I get very curious about what is excluded, abandoned, pushed out of view, out of sight. In the dictionary, it is never the meanings that are pushed aside. They always belong. Every dictionary has them. Has them with numbers. Has them in the main text. But there is "something else" sometimes, but always set off from the text, set off in parentheses. I'm referring, of course, to the *etymology* of the word. In parentheses, set off, as the dictionary itself says of the practice, set off as a digression, an interruption of continuity, an interval, an interlude, something independent and unnecessary to the surrounding text.

When I look up a meaning of a word I find that my imagination is not stirred. The meaning facilitates understanding the concept of the word and does this by talking about the word in other words. But this does not set my imagination going. I believe that much of our "explanatory," "interpretive," and "understanding" approaches to the dream image have a similar fate. It is not that they are not true. It is that they do not lead us to imagination's realm.

But if we get into the parentheses, inside those digressions, into those interruptions of continuity, those interludes, something else begins to happen. And just at this point a thought intrudes itself which should of course be in a parenthesis but I can't do it. I think just now of Jacques Derrida and his "deconstruction" approach, which in connection with these parentheses would have us turn them around facing the other way) (so that the main text is captured by these little enclosures and the digressions, the interludes, the interruptions are set free. But then you would ask: how could we have any rational discourse if we start breaking the rules that are so basic? Well is that the point? To have rational discourse? Or, might it not be to show what is there in one's experience, all of it, uncensored by parentheses? In fact, didn't depth psychology begin in an attempt to abolish parentheses—nothing excluded, everything belongs? I know that the simplest way to overcome writer's block is to forget parentheses all punctuation in fact as poetry has discovered and let everything have its say everything on equal footing the silly idea mingling with the most profound I once had a dream that I would have to write a paper on the importance of being silly—but I'm aware now that it's time to get back to order, to return the punctuation, to bring the parentheses back, to find the trail of rational discourse once again. I was getting close to breaking out with...but I "parenthe*seized*" it!

So what do we find in the parenthetical enclosure when we look at "explanation" in the dictionary? (Should I really consider that thought I just had that divided parenthetical into parent and hetical and noting that yes this parenthesis has to do with the word's parents, its parentage, but what in the world is this word "hetical"? It's not in any dictionary so it's obviously not a word. What do you mean it's not a word? It's right there: *hetical*. But what does it mean? I don't know. Let's make up a meaning for it, maybe something to do with what word parents do to create word offspring. You can't just make up a meaning like that. That's heretical. What? Are you trying to say there's some relation between hetical and heretical? Nonsense! Stop. Back to the point!) You can see how this craziness, this madness can get out of hand. Out of hand, yes. Comprehension. We must make sure we prehend together. That is, keep everything in our hands, together in our hands. That prehend means to seize and grasp in the hands. So let's not let things get out of hand.

So, what do we find when we finally get to the parenthesis in the word explain? We find first a reference to how the word appeared several hundred years ago during the time referred to as Middle English. And then explain was called "explanen." It says it was imported from the Latin word *explānāre* and is really two words: *ex-* meaning "completely," and *plānus,* meaning "plain" and "flat." We are then referred to its Indo-European root, *pele.* The basic sense of this root, from which many words develop, is "to spread out flat." The spirit of this word would be in opposition to wrinkles. That's why when we explain something we want to get the wrinkles out, to flatten out, make plane. Which is, of course, exactly opposite our wish in a story: there the wrinkle is essential, a story without a wrinkle is too plain. A story pulls us into its wrinkles, its twists, turns, folds. When a story unfolds completely we are left a bit sad, missing something of the tangle the story had drawn us into, wishing for another. Now we can learn something here about our approach to dreams or poems. We can fold ourselves into them, like that fabulous bird *pi i niao,* allow the wrinkles of the dream or poem to catch us and pull us into the story or we can try to take the wrinkles out and make plain. It is obvious that active imagination is a way of going into the story of the dream (or even a work of art), while treating the dream as an instance of another story (like a myth, for example), or relating the events in the dream to what we have done or might do, or accounting for the dream in other words, all this aims at taking the wrinkles, the story quality, out and making plain, explaining it. The same is true of a poem. The same with art. Have you ever done an active imagination with a painting, a sculpture, a poem? Or a novel? Modern novels are wonderful for this because modern novels do not end, they just stop as dreams do. Invitations, as it were, to carry on. "Dream the dream onward," Jung said.

Now all of this onward quality has a prospective character, that is, something to do with the future. One can explain something only by reducing it to or amplifying it toward something we already know, something we can number like the definitions in a dictionary. But this misses something quite essential and that something is contained in Jung's idea and feeling about the symbol-producing qualities of the psyche. He said often enough that a symbol was the best possible expression of something not yet fully known. We should never tire of hearing this, for it is what would animate our psychology and save it from the state of stony orthodoxy, if we could hear it deeply enough.

You never can know in advance where psyche will speak to you. But it pays to listen. One day as I was rushing, late, to see my analyst, as I was anxiously awaiting the elevator, I saw a sign painter at the window hand-painting a sign. I was curiously drawn to him and went over next to him. His first words to me were: "You will want to know this is a dying art. No one has time for it anymore. No one loves it enough. Not like Ghiberti. Ghiberti took twenty-five years with his doors." I wandered off down the street wondering who Ghiberti was, suddenly remembering my appointment with my analyst and now twenty minutes late! The sign painter was gone. But the sign he painted is still there. And five years later, almost at midnight, a stranger knocks at my door at the University where I'm frantically preparing to leave for Europe the next day and asks: "Is Dr. Lovejoy here?" And we look for my colleague but he's nowhere to be found. And two days later, after midnight, I'm in a bus riding from Pisa to Florence and the bus pulls over to the side to pick up someone whose car had stalled. Yes it was that man who had knocked at my door in Santa Barbara two nights before. We were struck by the strangeness of this connection. Because he had to leave Florence that day he said that the only thing he could think of to celebrate this event was to walk around Florence right then in the middle of the night to show me things that I must not miss seeing and that we would have to start with the doors on the Baptistry of St. John, the doors Ghiberti had labored on and loved and left to us.

It has taken me many years to listen to what psyche was saying in this string of curious events. It seems I've finally gotten the message psyche had delivered through that old sign painter. "It's about time" I hear her echo, and now I too agree.

Well, this has been my augury. I want to leave you with a hope, a feeling, and a poem. The hope is that for Jung's sake and to his honor I have not given a *Jungian* lecture in the usual sense. The feeling is that I love having had an audience with such willing ears to speak to for three evenings—and now an audience of readers as well. And the poem is Antonio Machado's little jewel, which I believe sums up in eleven words all I have said here with thousands:

> Between living and dreaming
> there is a third thing.
> Guess it.[123]

Notes

1. Nathan Schwartz-Salant, *Narcissism and Character Transforma-tion: The Psychology of Narcissistic Character Disorders* (Toronto: Inner City Books, 1982).

2. For a succinct statement of Hillman's archetypal psychology and a sampling of the relevant literature, see James Hillman, *Archetypal Psychology: A Brief Account* (Dallas: Spring Publications, 1983).

3. C. G. Jung, *Letters* (Princeton: Princeton University Press, 1975), II:549. To Miguel Serrano, 31 March 1960.

4. Ibid., 591. To Herbert Read, 2 September 1960.

5. Wolfgang Amadeus Mozart, "A Letter," in Brewster Ghiselin, ed., *The Creative Process: A Symposium* (New York: New American Library, 1952), 45.

6. The phrase is Hermann Paul's, as cited in Theodore Thass-Thienemann, *The Interpretation of Language* (New York: Aronson, 1968), I:81-82.

7. Not long at all: "...it may very well be that in another ten years people will pay ten thousand dollars in cash to be castrated, just in order to be affected by something." Wallace Shawn and André Gregory, *My Dinner with André: A Screenplay* (New York: Grove Press, 1981), 90.

8. As cited by Saul Bellow, "A World Too Much With Us," *Critical Inquiry* 1 (1975): 1-9. Bellow's reflections on Wordsworth's alarm are worth hearing more fully: "Wordsworth warned that we laid waste our powers by getting and spending. It is more serious than that now. Worse than getting and spending, modern distraction, worldwide irrationality, and madness threaten existence itself. We may not make it. Under the circumstances, I have no advice to offer other writers. I can only say,

speaking for myself, that the Heraclitean listening to the essence of things becomes more and more important."

9. As told by Longus in *Daphnis and Chloe* (Cambridge: Harvard University Press, 1916). For a further discussion of this theme see Russell A. Lockhart, "Psyche in Hiding," *Quadrant* 13 (1980): 83-87. Also important to a deeper sense of Echo is Pat Berry, *Echo's Subtle Body* (Dallas: Spring Publications, 1982), and Rafael Lopez-Pedraza, "The Tale of Dryops and the Birth of Pan: An Archetypal and Psychotherapeutic Approach to Eros Between Men," *Spring 1976*: 176-190.

10. C. G. Jung, *Memories, Dreams, Reflections* (New York: Random House, 1961), 192-193.

11. Jung, C. G. "Analytical Psychology and Education," in *The Collected Works of C. G. Jung* (Princeton: Princeton University Press, 1960), 17:173. This series will hereinafter be noted as *CW* with volume number (but not title unless a complete work), article title, and *paragraph* number referenced.

12. Russell A. Lockhart, "The Forgotten Psyche of Behavioral Therapy," *Psychological Perspectives* 4 (1973): 22-43.

13. Russell A. Lockhart, "Mary's Dog Is An Ear Mother: Listening To the Voices of Psychosis," *Psychological Perspectives* 6 (1975): 144-160.

14. C. G. Jung, "The Content of the Psychoses," *CW* 3:387.

15. Russell A. Lockhart, "Cancer in Myth and Dream: An Archetypal Perspective On the Relation Between Dreams and Disease," *Spring 1977*: 1-26.

16. Russell A. Lockhart, "Eros in Language, Myth and Dream," *Quadrant* 11 (1978): 41-68.

17. Russell A. Lockhart, "Words as Eggs," *Psychological Perspectives* 9 (1978): 57-83.

18. Lockhart, " Psyche in Hiding."

19. Lewis Carroll, *Through the Looking Glass and What Alice Found There*, in Martin Gardner, *The Annotated Alice* (New York: Bramhall House, 1960).

20. As quoted by Aniela Jaffé, "Symbolism in the Visual Arts," in C. G. Jung, ed., *Man and His Symbols* (Garden City: Doubleday, 1964), 254.

21. Russell A. Lockhart, "Coins and Psychological Change," in Russell A. Lockhart et al., *Soul and Money* (Dallas: Spring Publications, 1982).

22. The quotation from Pindar is from his funeral poetry preserved as a fragment (number 131) of a larger but lost work.

23. Since giving these lectures, we have moved further north, to the small town of Port Townsend, on the Olympic Peninsula, in Washington.

24. John Ashbery, "Catalpas," *Shadow Train* (New York: Penguin, 1981), 39.

25. From "The C. G. Jung Lectures," dated March 1980, a descriptive statement of the purpose and intention of the lectures accompanying the formal letter of invitation from the C. G. Jung Foundation for Analytical Psychology, Inc., of New York.

26. Federico Garcia Lorca, "Casida of the Rose," trans., Robert Bly, *News of the Universe: Poems of Twofold Consciousness* (San Francisco: Sierra Club Books, 1980), 109.

27. H. G. Baynes, *Mythology of the Soul* (London: Methuen and Co., 1949), 132.

28. Lewis Hyde, *The Gift: Imagination and the Erotic Life of Property* (New York: Random House, 1983).

29. Rainer Maria Rilke, from the 1914 poem "Turning Point": "Work of seeing is done,/ now practise heart-work/ upon those images captive within you...." Michael Hamburger's translation, quoted in Robert Bly, *Selected Poems of Rainer Maria Rilke* (New York: Harper, 1981), 157.

30. Jung, *Memories*, 353.

31. As quoted by Gaston Bachelard, *The Poetics of Reverie* (Boston: Beacon Press, 1969), 48.

32. Jung, *Letters*, II:119. To Aniela Jaffé, 29 May 1953.

33. Roland Barthes, *Camera Lucida: Reflections on Photography*, trans., Richard Howard (New York: Farrar, Straus and Giroux, 1981), 27.

34. Muriel Spark, "Created and Abandoned," *The New Yorker* (12 November 1979): 60.

35. The phrase is Hermann Paul's, as quoted by Thass-Thienemann, *The Interpretation of Language*, I:183.

36. Jonathan Schell, *The Fate of the Earth* (New York: Alfred A. Knopf, 1982).

37. *The Wall* (New York: American Broadcasting Company, 16 February 1982).

38. Barthes, *Camera Lucida*, 96, 117.

39. From the film *A Matter of Heart*, produced by the C. G. Jung Institute of Los Angeles.

40. Shawn and Gregory, *My Dinner with André*, 91-92.

41. Jung, *Letters*, I:469-470. To Aniela Jaffé, 8 July 1947.

42. Ibid., II:118. To James Kirsch, 28 May 1953.

43. Jung, *Memories,* 353.

44. Sigmund Freud, *Civilization and Its Discontents,* trans. Joan Riviere in *The Major Works of Sigmund Freud, Great Books of the Western World* (Chicago: Encyclopædia Britannica, 1952), vol. 54, 802.

45. Sigmund Freud, *New Introductory Lectures,* trans. W. J. H. Sprott (New York: W. W. Norton, 1965), 151. "Over the human mind" might also be translated as "over the human soul," if one follows Bettelheim's suggestion to translate the German word *seele* as "soul" rather than "mental life" as has been done in Freud translations. As Bettelheim notes, "mental life," has a perfectly good German equivalent (*geistig*), which Freud did not use. See Bruno Bettelheim, *Freud and Man's Soul* (New York: Knopf, 1983), 71-72.

46. Nikos Kazantzakis, *The Saviours of God,* trans. Kimon Friar (New York: Simon and Schuster, 1960), 106.

47. Jung, "Answer to Job," *CW* 11:686; *Memories,* 338.

48. Jung, *Memories,* 353.

49. Jung, *Letters,* II:591. To Herbert Read, 2 September 1960.

50. Wallace Stevens, "Not Ideas About the Thing But the Thing Itself," *The Collected Poems of Wallace Stevens* (New York: Alfred A. Knopf, 1980), 534.

51. C. G. Jung, *Dream Analysis* (Princeton: Princeton University Press, 1984), 69.

52. Gaston Bachelard, *The Poetics of Reverie,* trans. Daniel Russell (Boston: Beacon Press, 1969), 49.

53. Hermann Paul's expression as quoted by Thass-Thienemann, *The Interpretation of Language,* I:81-82.

54. Jung, *Dream Analysis,* 69-70, 71.

55. Jaun Ramón Jiménez, "The Well," *Platero and I: An Andalusian Elegy 1907-1916* (Boulder: Shambala, 1978), 59.

56. Jiménez, *Platero,* 59.

57. As quoted by Bachelard, *Poetics of Reverie,* 48.

58. C. G. Jung, "The Structure of the Unconscious," *CW* 7:494. Here I've used Jung's first expression of this idea (published in 1916) because of its proximity in time with his confrontation with the unconscious (Jung, *Memories,* 170-199), which I believe determined Jung's unique view of the symbol.

59. Ralph Waldo Emerson, "The Poet," *Essays and Lectures* (New York: The Library of Americana, 1983), 455.

60. Rainer Maria Rilke, "Sonnets to Orpheus," trans. Robert Bly *Selected Poems of Rainer Maria Rilke* (New York: Harper & Row, 1981), 197.

61. As quoted by Jaffé, "Symbolism in the Visual Arts," 263.

62. It should not go unnoticed that in this phrase from Jung's letter to Herbert Read the word "dream" is capitalized. Read's reply (Jung, *Letters*, II:591, n. 8) also used the capital form in speaking of the artist's "longing to be put in touch with the Dream, that is to say...the future." The emphasis is not on the ego's *predicting* the future—using dreams for power—but on man's conscious reflection and eros involvement in responding to the images bearing the incipient future in such a way as to participate *with* God in the birth of the manifest future. As Jung wrote, "Everything psychic is pregnant with the future" (C. G. Jung, *CW* 14:53).

63. The expression is Klee's as quoted by Jaffé, "Symbolism in the Visual Arts," 263.

64. Jung, *Letters*, II:590.

65. Geoffrey H. Hartman, *Saving the Text* (Baltimore: The Johns Hopkins University Press, 1981).

66. Artemas Packard, *The Orozco Frescoes at Dartmouth*, Albert I. Dickerson, ed. (Dartmouth: Trustees of Dartmouth College, 1962). Comment accompanying the twelfth panel entitled "Gods of the Modern World."

67. We might do well to listen to Jung's advice: "Therefore anyone who wants to know the human psyche....would be better advised to...bid farewell to his study, and wander with human heart through the world. There, in the horrors of prisons, lunatic asylums and hospitals, in drab suburban pubs, in brothels, and gambling-hells, in the salons of the elegant, the Stock Exchanges, Socialist meetings, churches, revivalist gatherings and ecstatic sects, through love and hate, through the experience of passion in every form in his own body, he would reap richer stores of knowledge than text-books a foot thick could give him, and he will know how to doctor the sick with real knowledge of the human soul." (C. G. Jung, *CW* 7:409.).

68. AE, *The Candle of Vision* (Wheaton: The Theosophical Publishing House, 1974). Adler's note reads: "Perhaps the fantasy figure personifying the dark aspect of the unconscious, destructive and creative at once, described in Jung's earliest childhood dream (*Memories*, pp. 11ff./25 ff., esp. p. 15/29). Many years later he encountered a parallel figure, the pilgrim of eternity, in *The Candle of Vision* (1920) by the Irish

poet A.E. (George W. Russell), which impressed him profoundly." In Jung, *Letters*, II:590, n. 6.

69. Leslie Shepard, "Introduction," in AE, *The Candle of Vision*, iii.

70. AE, *The Candle of Vision*, 71-72. Later, Russell signed one of his articles "AEON" in honor of this early experience. A proofreader could not understand it and on the manuscript wrote "AE--?" Russell responded by adopting the initials and thereafter published under this accidental pseudonym.

71. AE, Ibid., 73.

72. "Freud's method is an artist's method." Havelock Ellis, in Sigmund Freud, "A Note on the Prehistory of the Techniques of Analysis," James Strachey ed., *Sigmund Freud: Collected Papers* (New York: Basic Books, 1959), V:102. "The theory itself is in fact nothing but the kind of psychology used by poets." Alfred von Bergner, in Ernest Jones, *The Life and Work of Sigmund Freud* (New York: Basic Books, 1953), I:253.

73. For another perspective see Russell A. Lockhart, "What Whale Does America Pursue?" *Words as Eggs* (Dallas: Spring Publications, 1983), 79-84. Even as early as 1922, Jung wrote: "Art...has no 'meaning,'...it is like nature, which simply *is*....It needs no meaning, for meaning has nothing to do with art." C. G. Jung, "On the Relation of Analytical Psychology to Poetry," *CW* 15:77.

74. Rafael Lopez-Pedraza, as quoted by Pat Berry, "An Approach to the Dream," *Spring 1974*: 61.

75. James Hillman, *The Dream and the Underworld* (New York: Harper & Row, 1979).

76. Theodore Roethke, "The Restored," *The Collected Poems of Theodore Roethke* (Garden City: Anchor Press, 1975), 241. Quoted as in the original.

77. Jung, *Letters* I:226. To Martin Elsasser, 28 January 1937.

78. Ibid., 469. To Esther Harding, 8 July 1947.

79. Ibid. II:512. To Lloyd W. Wolf, 25 July 1959.

80. Jung, *Memories*, 192.

81. Ibid., 192.

82. Ibid., 190-191.

83. Ibid., 191.

84. Ibid.

85. The most readily available edition of "The Seven Sermons to the Dead" is to be found in Appendix V of the paperback edition of Jung's *Memories*. It was not included in the hardback edition.

86. Jung, *Memories*, 192.

87. Ibid., 185.

88. Ibid.

89. Ibid.

90. Ibid.

91. Ibid., 181.

92. Ibid., 182.

93. The full influence of Lou Andreas-Salomé on Jung has yet to be essayed fully. As initial background in this difficult territory, see Karl H. Abenheimer, "Lou Andreas-Salomé's Main Contribution to Psycho-Analysis," *Spring 1971*: 22-37.

94. It now also appears for a certainty that the woman referred to was Sabina Spielrein, an early patient of Jung's who later became a psychoanalyst. The complex relationship between Spielrein, Freud, and Jung has come to light with the discovery of Spielrein's diaries and letters. This material is presented and examined in detail in Aldo Carotenuto, *A Secret Symmetry: Sabina Spielrein—Between Jung and Freud* (New York: Pantheon, 1982). This book, available to me only after the lectures, raises serious questions which cannot be taken up here but which will be obvious to the reader.

95. Jung, *Memories*, 185.

96. Ibid., 185-186.

97. Ibid., 187.

98. Ibid.

99. Ibid.

100. For a beautiful treatment of this first appearance of the anima, unavailable to me at the time of the lectures, see James Hillman, "Thought of the Heart," *Eranos Lectures* 2 (Dallas: Spring Publications, 1981): 34-37.

101. C. G. Jung, *Word and Image*, ed. Aniela Jaffé (Princeton: Princeton University Press, 1979), 194. Adler's translation is: "Let the light I have carried in my womb shine forth." (Jung, *Letters* II:616.) The term *alvo* (from *alvus*) is most literally "womb." The term *gestavi* is from *gesto* which derives from *gero* meaning, literally, "to be pregnant," and is preserved in the English use of "to carry" a child in reference to pregnancy. The past tense (have carried, have borne) indicates the birth has taken place.

102. A picture of the stone carving may be found in Jung, *Letters*-II:617 and in Jung, *Word and Image*, 194.

103. Jung, *Letters* II:615-616. To Ignanz Tauber, 13 December 1960.

104. See Maud Oakes, *The Stone Speaks* (Wilmette: Chiron Publications, 1987).

105. All quotations from Jung, *Letters* II:615-616.

106. Marilyn Nagy, review of *The Moon and the Virgin: Reflections on the Archetypal Feminine* by Nor Hall, *Quadrant* 14/2 (1981): 111.

107. Nor Hall, *The Moon and the Virgin: Reflections on the Archetypal Feminine* (New York: Harper & Row, 1980).

108. Jung, *Letters* II:616, n. 4.

109. Harold Rosenberg, "Metaphysical Feelings in Modern Art," *Critical Inquiry* 2 (1975): 232.

110. Jung, *Letters* II:605.

111. Ibid.

112. C. G. Jung, *Visions* (Zurich: Spring Publications, 1976), II:284.

113. The reader, if not familiar with the poetry of Sorley MacLean, will be pleased to discover his work. See his poem "The Selling of A Soul," in Sorley MacLean, *Spring Tide and Neap Tide: Selected Poems 1932-72* (Edinburgh: Canongate Publishing Ltd., 1977), 16-18.

114. Three books have been published thus far: Janet Dallett, *Midnight's Daughter* (Port Townsend: The Lockhart Press, 1983); Marc Hudson, *Journal for An Injured Son* (Port Townsend: The Lockhart Press, 1985); Peter Levitt, *Homage: Leda As Virgin* (Port Townsend: The Lockhart Press, 1986).

115. Rainer Maria Rilke, *The Notebooks of Malte Laurids Brigge*: "And still it is not enough to have memories. One must be able to forget them when they are many and one must have the patience to wait until they come again. For it is not yet the memories themselves. Not till they have turned to blood within us, to glance and gesture, nameless and no longer to be distinguished from ourselves—not till then can it happen that in a most rare hour the first word of a verse arises in their midst and goes forth from them." Quoted by John J. L. Mood, *Rilke On Love and Other Difficulties* (New York: Norton, 1975), 94.

116. Carl Kerenyi, *The Heroes of the Greeks* (New York: Grove Press, 1960).

117. AE, *A Candle of Vision*, 75-76.

118. Ibid., 98-100.

119. Ibid., 100-101.

120. Jung, *Letters* I:298. To Mary Mellon, 18 April 1934.

121. Ibid. I:172. To James Kirsch, 29 September 1934.

122. Edwin Muir, *An Autobiography* (London: Hogarth Press, 1954), 89.

123. Antonio Machado, *The Dream Below the Sun*, trans. Willis Barnstone (Trumansburg: The Crossing Press, 1981), 109.

Bibliography

AE, *The Candle of Vision*. Wheaton: The Theosophical Publishing House, 1974.

A Matter of Heart. Los Angeles: C. G. Jung Institute of Los Angeles, 1985.

Abenheimer, Karl H. "Lou Andreas-Salomé's Main Contribution to Psycho-Analysis," *Spring 1971*: 22-37.

Ashbery, John. *Shadow Train*. New York: Penguin, 1981.

Bachelard, Gaston. *The Poetics of Reverie*. Translated by Daniel Russell. Boston: Beacon Press, 1969.

Barthes, Roland. *Camera Lucida: Reflections on Photography*. Translated by Richard Howard. New York: Farrar, Straus and Giroux, 1981.

Baynes, H. G. *Mythology of the Soul*. London: Methuen and Co., 1949.

Bellow, Saul. "A World Too Much With Us." *Critical Inquiry* 1 (1975): 1-9.

Berry, Pat. "An Approach to the Dream," *Spring 1974*: 58-79.

———. *Echo's Subtle Body*. Dallas: Spring Publications, 1982.

Bruno Bettelheim. *Freud and Man's Soul*. New York: Knopf, 1983.

Bly, Robert. *News of the Universe: Poems of Twofold Consciousness*. San Francisco: Sierra Club Books, 1980.

———. *Selected Poems of Rainer Maria Rilke*. New York: Harper, 1981.

Carotenuto, Aldo. *A Secret Symmetry: Sabina Spielrein—Between Jung and Freud*. New York: Pantheon, 1982.

Carroll, Lewis. *Through the Looking Glass and What Alice Found There*. In *The Annotated Alice*, edited by Martin Gardner. New York: Bramhall House, 1960.

Emerson, Ralph Waldo. *Essays and Lectures*. New York: The Library of Americana, 1983.

Freud, Sigmund. *Civilization and Its Discontents.* In *The Major Works of Sigmund Freud,* translated by Joan Riviere. *Great Books of the Western World.* Vol. 54. Chicago: Encyclopædia Britannica, 1952.

———. *New Introductory Lectures.* Translated by W. J. H. Sprott. New York: W. W. Norton, 1965.

———. "A Note on the Prehistory of the Techniques of Analysis," In *Sigmund Freud: Collected Papers,* edited by James Strachey. 5 vols. New York: Basic Books, 1959.

Ghiselin, Brewster, ed. *The Creative Process: A Symposium.* New York: New American Library, 1952.

Hall, Nor. *The Moon and the Virgin: Reflections on the Archetypal Feminine.* New York: Harper & Row, 1980.

Hartman, Geoffrey H. *Saving the Text.* Baltimore: The Johns Hopkins University Press, 1981.

Hillman, James. *Archetypal Psychology: A Brief Account.* Dallas: Spring Publications, 1983.

———. *The Dream and the Underworld.* New York: Harper & Row, 1979.

———. "Thought of the Heart." *Eranos Lectures* 2. Dallas: Spring Publications, 1981.

Hyde, Lewis. *The Gift: Imagination and the Erotic Life of Property.* New York: Random House, 1983.

Jaffé, Aniela. "Symbolism in the Visual Arts." In C. G. Jung, ed. *Man and His Symbols.* Garden City: Doubleday, 1964.

Jiménez, Jaun Ramón. *Platero and I: An Andalusian Elegy 1907-1916.* Boulder: Shambala, 1978.

Jones, Ernest. *The Life and Work of Sigmund Freud.* 3 vols. New York: Basic Books, 1953.

Jung, C. G. *The Collected Works* (Bollingen Series XX). 20 vols. Translated by R. F. C. Hull. Edited by Herbert Read, Michael Fordham, Gerhard Adler, William McGuire. Princeton: Princeton University Press, 1953-1979.

———. *Dream Analysis.* Princeton: Princeton University Press, 1984.

———. *Letters.* 2 vols. Princeton: Princeton University Press, 1975.

———. *Memories, Dreams, Reflections.* New York: Random House, 1961.

———. *Visions.* 2 vols. Zurich: Spring Publications, 1976.

———. *Word and Image.* Edited by Aniela Jaffé. Princeton: Princeton University Press, 1979.

Kazantzakis, Nikos. *The Saviours of God.* Translated by Kimon Friar. New York: Simon and Schuster, 1960.

Kerenyi, Carl. *The Heroes of the Greeks*. New York: Grove Press, 1960.

Lockhart, Russell A. *Words As Eggs: Psyche in Language and Clinic*. Dallas: Spring Publications, 1983.

—————. "Cancer in Myth and Dream: An Archetypal Perspective On the Relation Between Dreams and Disease." *Spring 1977*: 1-26.

—————. "Coins and Psychological Change." In Russell A. Lockhart et al., *Soul and Money*. Dallas: Spring Publications, 1982.

—————. "Eros in Language, Myth and Dream." *Quadrant* 11 (1978): 41-68.

—————. "The Forgotten Psyche of Behavioral Therapy." *Psychological Perspectives* 4 (1973): 22-43.

—————. "Mary's Dog Is An Ear Mother: Listening To the Voices of Psychosis." *Psychological Perspectives* 6 (1975): 144-160.

—————. "Psyche in Hiding." *Quadrant* 13 (1980): 76-105.

—————. "What Whale Does America Pursue?" *Psychological Perspectives* 10 (1979): 83-87.

—————. "Words as Eggs." *Psychological Perspectives* 9 (1978): 57-83.

Longus. *Daphnis and Chloe*. Cambridge: Harvard University Press, 1916.

Lopez-Pedraza, Rafael. "The Tale of Dryops and the Birth of Pan: An Archetypal and Psychotherapeutic Approach to Eros Between Men." *Spring 1976*: 176-190.

Machado, Antonio. *The Dream Below the Sun*. Translated by Willis Barnstone. Trumansburg: The Crossing Press, 1981.

MacLean, Sorley. *Spring Tide and Neap Tide: Selected Poems 1932-72*. Edinburgh: Canongate Publishing Ltd., 1977.

Mood, John J. L. *Rilke On Love and Other Difficulties*. New York: Norton, 1975.

Muir, Edwin. *An Autobiography*. London: Hogarth Press, 1954.

Nagy, Marilyn. Review of *The Moon and the Virgin: Reflections on the Archetypal Feminine*, by Nor Hall. *Quadrant* 14/2 (1981): 108-111.

Oakes, Maud. *The Stone Speaks*. Wilmette: Chiron Publications, 1987.

Packard, Artemas. *The Orozco Frescoes at Dartmouth*. Edited by Albert I. Dickerson. Dartmouth: Trustees of Dartmouth College, 1962.

Roethke, Theodore. *The Collected Poems of Theodore Roethke*. Garden City: Anchor Press, 1975.

Rosenberg, Harold. "Metaphysical Feelings in Modern Art." *Critical Inquiry* 2 (1975): 217-232.

Schell, Jonathan. *The Fate of the Earth*. New York: Alfred A. Knopf, 1982.

Schwartz-Salant, Nathan. *Narcissism and Character Transformation: The Psychology of Narcissistic Character Disorders.* Toronto: Inner City Books, 1982.

Shawn, Wallace and André Gregory. *My Dinner with André: A Screenplay.* New York: Grove Press, 1981.

Spark, Muriel. "Created and Abandoned." *The New Yorker* (12 November 1979): 60.

Stevens, Wallace. *The Collected Poems of Wallace Stevens.* New York: Alfred A. Knopf, 1980.

Thass-Thienemann, Theodore. *The Interpretation of Language.* 2 vols. New York: Aronson, 1968.

The Wall. New York: American Broadcasting Company, 16 February 1982.

Index